CopyKat.com's

Dining Out
at Home
Cookbook

2

Stephanie Manley

CopyKat.com's

Dining Out at Home Cookbook 2

More Recipes for the Most Delicious Dishes
from America's Most Popular Restaurants

Ulysses Press

Published by Ulysses Press
P.O. Box 3440
Berkeley, CA 94703
www.ulyssespress.com

ISBN: 978-1-61243-181-9
Library of Congress Catalog Number 2013931788

Printed in Canada by Marquis Book Printing

10 9 8 7 6 5 4 3 2 1

Acquisitions Editor: Keith Riegert
Managing Editor: Claire Chun
Editor: Phyllis Elving
Proofreader: Lauren Harrison
Production: Jake Flaherty, Lindsay Tamura
Cover design: Lakia Ross
Interior design: what!design @ whatweb.com
Interior icons: ©shutterstock.com/Massimo Sairezzo, Harjis A, Seller, Miguel Angel Salinas Salinas, svidenovic, blondinkadesign, Tancha, Mikateke, nata_danilenko
Cover photos: coffee drink: © Dreamstime.com/Andrei Levitskiy, fried chicken: ©shutterstock.com/MSPhotographic, pasta fagioli: ©shutterstock.com/Robyn Mackenzie

Distributed by Publishers Group West

To my mom, Grandma McDowell, Grandma Eynard, Denise, and Bella. All of you have inspired me in so many ways. You have taught me to cook and enabled my creative spirit through your encouragement. I am deeply grateful for all you have given me.

Contents

Note to the Reader

CopyKat.com's Dining Out at Home Cookbook 2 is a collection of original recipes created by the author, Stephanie Manley, for the preparation of food items that taste like the ones available from many of America's favorite restaurants and food brands.

All trademarks that appear in recipe titles, ingredient lists, and elsewhere in this book belong to their respective owners and are mentioned here for informational purposes only. Every effort has been made to identify third-party trademarks with the "®" or "™" symbols, as appropriate. No sponsorship or endorsement of this book by, and no affiliation with, the trademark owners is claimed or suggested.

The author encourages her readers to patronize the restaurants and food manufacturers in order to find out for themselves what the authentic versions of these food items taste like!

Let's Go Make a Memory

※※※※※※※※※※※※※※※※※※※※

I have been writing CopyKat recipes for a long time. I started my website, CopyKat.com, back in 1995. Initially it was a place to keep my own family recipes. Maybe you have a shoebox, a drawer, or a notebook where you store recipes. My mother filed some of hers in a binder she'd once used for a sorority she belonged to.

Many of my favorite moments in life took place around a table, involving food. I can remember sitting at my great-grandmother's table as a small child when she served sauerkraut and potatoes. Her sauerkraut was homemade, meaning she made it from cabbage, salt, and time. It tasted amazing. I remember one time Mom and I were getting into a heated discussion about just how much of it I was going to eat, when whatever I was drinking got knocked over and spilled everywhere.

I can also remember cooking with my dad's mother, and she was so neat and tidy. She would be shocked and horrified if she walked into my kitchen now, as messy as it sometimes is. Her pies and cakes were also neat. She was always trying out a recipe, and I always wanted to her to write down her recipes for me to take home.

My parents and I moved a lot when I was growing up because of Dad's work in retail management. We got to move around and meet new people. In meeting new people, you get to try new food. On my website you'll find peanut butter cookies, apple pie, and other goodies from neighbors we had when I was growing up. Just thinking about those baked goods reminds me of wonderful times I had with those people.

I was off to college and met more wonderful friends. Denise taught me how to make wine jelly and so much more, so thinking about wine jelly always makes me feel young, as if I were in college again. All the while I was collecting recipes. Then came the Internet, so in 1995 I began to post recipes online. I really only did it for myself, to make sure I'd be able to find my recipes. It's amazing how I began to think of recipes from other people as my personal recipes; they aren't mine per se, but the memories they evoke are wonderful.

I began to post re-creations of restaurant recipes. When I was in high school, we lived in a rural area—I mean, we lived off a dirt road and our TV came to us via a large antennae that you had to rotate when you wanted to watch a particular show. Sometimes we'd go into town to eat at a restaurant, and I wanted to re-create those recipes at home. The first two recipes that would launch what I do now were the Olive Garden Alfredo sauce and sweet and sour sauce. Alfredo sauce was something magical; we'd never had such a sauce on pasta when I was growing up. And sweet and sour sauce never tasted the same as at a restaurant when it came out of jar. So I began by reading all the cookbooks we had, and then all the cookbooks at the local library. I'd then try out recipes until I felt I had it right. Who knew that going to the Olive Garden would turn into something that I've done now for almost 20 years? I re-create restaurant recipes.

What makes restaurant meals so special? I think part of it is the memories you associate with them. Many of us go out to eat for birthdays and other celebrations, and we go with other people. It is sitting at a table breaking bread together that makes these meals special. And during these special meals we form new favorite dishes. It might be a special piece of cheesecake ordered for making straight A's. It might be a wonderful cocktail to toast a promotion. Or it could be just celebrating that the mail arrived that day!

So it is with great care that I re-create these recipes for you and your family. While we can't always recapture the moment we shared with those we love, we can re-create the food we had. I hope these recipes will bring you much happiness and more good memories to come.

Icon Guide

 AUTHOR FAVORITE

 COCKTAIL PARTY

 DINNER FOR ONE

 DINNER FOR TWO

 GAME DAY

 IMPRESS THE GUEST

 MAKE AHEAD

 MEAT LOVERS

 QUICK AND EASY

 SPICY

 VEGETARIAN

Drinks

When dining out, it's a treat to order a special drink. Whether this is a nonalcoholic beverage such as a fancy lemonade or a cocktail that you don't normally make at home, it's a pleasure to have someone prepare something special for you. Many of these fancy drinks can be made at home, too, letting you turn any moment into a celebratory occasion.

In this chapter I will show you how you can make exotic cocktails such as a Brazilian caipirinha, a wonderful citrus drink that's perfect for a summer day, and a fancy coffee like the ones you find at specialty coffee shops. Together, we're going to turn your kitchen into your favorite bar and your favorite coffee place.

Caipirinha

Fogo de Chao is a Brazilian-style barbecue restaurant with locations in many major cities. An endless supply of meat comes your way, so if you're a meat lover you'll feel as if you've died and gone to heaven. This is an all-you-can-eat restaurant, with more than 20 different varieties of meat served at any time. There's a top-notch salad bar with buffalo mozzarella, artichoke hearts, and so much more. Fogo de Chao also happens to have one of the best bars you'll ever find. Their house specialty is the caipirinha, made from cachaça liquor—a by-product of sugar making also known as Brazilian white rum. If you cannot find cachaça, a light rum will also work.

1 lime

2 tablespoons simple syrup (recipe on page 194) or 2 teaspoons superfine sugar

2 (1½-ounce) jiggers cachaça

club soda or lemon-lime soda (optional)

Wash and quarter the lime. Cut away the membrane at the center of each quarter and slice each quarter in half. Place the lime pieces in an old-fashioned cocktail glass and use a muddler to mash them. Add the simple syrup or superfine sugar and ice to fill the glass three-quarters full. Pour in the cachaça and stir gently. You can top off the drink with a bit of club soda or lemon-lime soda to completely fill the glass, if you wish.

◇◇◇◇◇◇◇◇◇◇◇◇◇◇◇◇◇◇◇◇◇◇
YIELD: 1 SERVING

TIP: Did you know that you can make your own superfine sugar in a food processor? Simply process regular granulated sugar in short pulses for approximately 15 to 20 seconds. Superfine sugar dissolves almost instantly in liquids.

CopyKat.com's **GRAND LUX CAFE®**

Strawberry Bellini

The Grand Lux Cafe is owned by the Cheesecake Factory, and the two restaurant chains share innovative menu items with superior taste and quality. Places that offer brunch don't always offer new and creative cocktails, but this strawberry Bellini is a wonderful take on your standard Bellini. Instead of using peach purée they use triple sec, an orange-flavored liqueur.

1 tablespoon finely diced strawberries, plus a strawberry for garnish (optional)

1 teaspoon triple sec

4 ounces Champagne or other sparkling wine

Place the diced strawberries in the bottom of a champagne flute. Add the triple sec, then slowly pour in the Champagne. Be careful not to fill the flute too quickly, or it may overflow. Add a strawberry for garnish if you wish.

YIELD: 1 SERVING

TIP: Buy inexpensive Champagne/sparkling wine for this recipe. Since liquor is being added, it isn't critical to buy anything that costs more than $10. I've had great luck with very inexpensive domestic sparkling wines that are under $5 a bottle.

CopyKat.com's **FATBURGER®**

Banana Shake

At Fatburger, the banana shakes are topped with whipped cream before serving.

- 2 cups premium vanilla ice cream
- 3 tablespoons half-and-half (or you can use milk)

- 2 teaspoons instant banana pudding powder

In a blender, combine the ice cream, half-and-half, and pudding powder. Blend until thick and creamy.

YIELD: APPROXIMATELY 2½ CUPS, OR 1 SERVING

TIP: This shake also works well with light ice cream. If you are diabetic, you may want to use sugar-free pudding and ice cream.

CopyKat.com's JACK IN THE BOX®

Eggnog Shake

So many of our favorite restaurants have seasonal menu items, and Jack in the Box offers a wonderful Eggnog Shake during the winter holidays. What I love the most about their shake is that they use a high-quality ice cream, making for a wonderfully rich and thick shake that's difficult to beat.

1 cup premium vanilla ice cream

⅓ cup eggnog (Bordon's Premium is highly recommended)

whipped cream and freshly grated nutmeg (optional)

Combine the ice cream and eggnog in a blender, and mix until well combined. If you wish, top your shake with whipped cream and a dash of freshly grated nutmeg.

YIELD: 1 SERVING

Caramel Frappé

When I asked the followers of CopyKat.com what McDonald's coffee drink at McDonald's was their favorite, the Caramel Frappé was by far the winner. If you don't have an espresso maker, make your coffee extra strong by using one and a half times the amount of coffee you'd would normally use in your drip maker.

2 servings espresso or 6 ounces strong coffee, chilled

1 tablespoon simple syrup (recipe on page 194)

½ cup nonfat milk

2 tablespoons caramel topping, divided

1 to 1½ cups crushed ice

whipped cream, for garnish

In a blender, combine the espresso or coffee, simple syrup, milk, 1 tablespoon caramel topping, and ice. Blend until the mixture is smooth and creamy. Pour into a glass. Add whipped cream, and drizzle the remaining 1 tablespoon caramel topping over the whipped cream.

YIELD: 1 SERVING

CopyKat.com's MCDONALD'S®

Frozen Strawberry Lemonade

Over the last few years, McDonald's has really increased its drink offerings. This strawberry lemonade is made with strawberry ice cream topping and lemonade mix. It's a tangy and sweet drink that's perfect on a hot afternoon.

2 cups prepared lemonade
(Country Time powdered drink mix
works well for this)

2 cups ice cubes

2 tablespoons strawberry ice cream
topping

Place the prepared lemonade and the ice cubes in a blender and blend until the ice is completely crushed. Spoon the strawberry ice cream topping into the bottom of 2 tall glasses and then pour the frozen lemonade over it.

YIELD: 2 SERVINGS

CopyKat.com's MCDONALD'S®

Strawberry Banana Smoothie

Sometimes the drive-thru line can be really long, and you may be running short on time. But you can put this smoothie together in just a couple of minutes at home. It combines fresh bananas, frozen strawberries, and yogurt to make a drink you can have for breakfast.

1 cup crushed ice

½ cup sliced banana

2 tablespoons vanilla yogurt

1 (10-ounce) package frozen sliced strawberries (about 1¼ cups)

Place the ice, sliced banana, yogurt, and sliced strawberries in a blender. Blend on the purée setting until the mixture is smooth and creamy.

YIELD: 2 SERVINGS

CopyKat.com's **OLIVE GARDEN®**

Berry Sangria

Dining out means enjoying something extra-special with your meal, and sometimes that means a fun drink. Olive Garden's Berry Sangria is a real treat—wine that's sweetened and served with fresh berries. While the Olive Garden doesn't add club soda to their sangria, if you wish you can add a little to give yours a refreshing fizz. If fresh blackberries or blueberries aren't in season, frozen berries work well.

1 (750 ml) bottle red wine (I use merlot)

2 cups cran-raspberry juice

¼ cup simple syrup (recipe on page 194)

2 cups fresh berries (such as strawberries, blackberries, or blueberries), for garnish

Combine the wine, juice, and simple syrup in a large pitcher, and stir well to combine. Let the mixture sit for a couple of hours before serving. Place ice into the glasses, then fresh fruit and the sangria. Garnish each glass with a whole berry.

YIELD: 6 SERVINGS

CopyKat.com's SONIC®

Vanilla Coke

One happy hour I love is at Sonic. Half-price drinks are enough to make my car veer immediately into the drive-thru. So are their vanilla Cokes. Sure, Coca-Cola makes a vanilla coke that you can purchase, but to me, one that's freshly made always tastes better. This vanilla syrup is great for making vanilla Coke, vanilla Dr. Pepper, and your favorite fancy coffee drink.

VANILLA SYRUP

1 cup water

2 cups sugar

1½ teaspoons vanilla extract

VANILLA COKE

2 to 3 teaspoons vanilla syrup

ice cubes, if desired

1½ cups (12 ounces) Coca-Cola

TO MAKE THE VANILLA SYRUP: In a small saucepan over medium heat, heat the water and sugar, stirring, until the sugar is dissolved. Stir in the vanilla extract. Let cool and store in an airtight container in the refrigerator.

TO MAKE A VANILLA COKE: Pour the vanilla syrup into a tall glass, add ice if desired, and finally pour in the soda. Use a long spoon to gently mix the vanilla flavor into the soda.

YIELD: 1 SERVING

CopyKat.com's SONIC®

Root Beer Freeze

Sonic offers so many different drink combinations that the total number is easily over 100,000. We know what a shake is, milk and ice cream combined. Well, one of my favorites is the freeze, and here we start with ice cream and then stop at the soda fountain. I'm partial to the root beer freeze. If you love a good old-fashioned root beer float, you'll want to prepare this drink. Now, you don't have to stop at just root beer, you can make this with Coca-Cola, Dr. Pepper, or any other soda that you like. You can also add in flavorings; a cherry Dr. Pepper freeze has always had a special place in my heart.

2 cups vanilla ice cream	½ cup root beer

Place the ice cream and root beer in a blender and purée for about 30 seconds. That's it.

YIELD: 1 LARGE FREEZE

CopyKat.com's **STARBUCKS™**

Eggnog Latte

How do you know the holidays have arrived? Well, one sign is that Starbucks brings out those red cups and many seasonal menu items. An eggnog latte has been one of my favorites for years. I recommend serving this topped with a light sprinkling of freshly grated nutmeg.

½ cup milk

½ cup eggnog

2 servings espresso or very strong coffee

whipped cream and freshly grated nutmeg, if desired

Heat together the milk and eggnog for about 1 minute in the microwave. Froth the milk mixture with a milk frother; if you don't have one of those, you can pour the milk into a blender and whirl it for about 30 seconds. If you don't have a blender, you can shake your milk mixture in a jar or even a cocktail shaker for about 1 minute. The milk will froth up and almost double in size.

Pour a serving of espresso or coffee into each of 2 coffee cups. Top each serving with half the frothed milk and eggnog. Add whipped cream and grated nutmeg, if you wish.

YIELD: 2 SERVINGS

Pumpkin Spice Latte

Who wants to wait until October every year to enjoy this coffee? Yes, you can get pumpkin-spiced coffee, but nothing tastes quite like a Starbucks Pumpkin Spice Latte. For this recipe, you start by making a pumpkin-spiced syrup. That's what makes the coffee taste so good.

PUMPKIN SYRUP

2½ cups water

1 tablespoon grated nutmeg

3 cinnamon sticks or 1½ tablespoons ground cinnamon

½-inch piece of fresh ginger or ½ teaspoon ground ginger

1 cup sugar

3 tablespoons canned pumpkin

PUMPKIN SPICE LATTE SERVING

½ cup espresso or strong coffee

2 to 3 tablespoons pumpkin syrup

½ cup milk, warmed and frothed*

whipped cream and freshly grated nutmeg, if desired

TO MAKE THE PUMPKIN SYRUP: Bring the water, nutmeg, cinnamon, and ginger to a boil in a medium saucepan. Turn down the heat and simmer for 20 minutes, then strain through a coffee filter. You want the seasoned water to be free of the spices. Pour the strained water back into the pan and add the sugar and pumpkin; mix well. Simmer for another 10 minutes. This will make about 1 pint of pumpkin spice syrup. Store the extra syrup in an airtight container in the refrigerator; it will stay fresh for up to a week.

TO MAKE THE LATTE: Brew a 4-ounce serving of espress or strong coffee. Place 2 to 3 tablespoons of pumpkin syrup in a coffee cup and then add the coffee. Gently pour the frothed milk over the coffee, and gently stir. If desired, top with whipped cream and a dash of nutmeg.

YIELD: 1 SERVING

TIP: If you don't have an espresso maker, simply make strong coffee by adding half again as much coffee as usual to your coffee maker. If you have a coffee grinder, grind your coffee fine to help it pick up more flavor.

NOTE: For how to froth milk, see the Starbucks Eggnog Latte recipe on page 16.

Ultimate Mojito

T.G.I. Friday's is known for having a good bar filled with innovative drinks. I love that they go the extra mile when preparing cocktails, always using really good ingredients. I think the cane sugar used in this mojito adds a nice flavor.

club soda

2 teaspoons superfine cane sugar (C&H makes superfine cane sugar)

6 or 7 fresh mint leaves, divided

2 teaspoons lime juice

2 ounces Bacardi rum

ice cubes

Pour a splash of club soda in the bottom of a highball glass (this is the tall and skinny cocktail glass). Add the sugar and 4 or 5 mint leaves; muddle the sugar into the mint. (If you don't have a muddler, you can use a wooden spoon.) Add the lime juice and rum to the glass and give it a quick stir. Add enough ice to fill the glass halfway and then top with more club soda; stir to mix well. Garnish the drink with another mint leaf or 2.

YIELD: 1 SERVING

Piña Colada Frutista Freeze

Who doesn't love a piña colada? For sipping while lying by the beach, I can't think of a more perfect drink. Creamy coconut combined with tangy sweet pineapple will always bring back good memories of lazy summer days. Taco Bell manages to capture this in a nonalcoholic version you can get at the drive-thru. The added fizz of lemon-lime soda makes this drink really sparkle.

½ cup ice

½ cup piña colada mix

¼ cup Sierra Mist or other lemon-lime soda

1 lime slice

Place the ice, piña colada mix, and soda in the blender and blend until the ice has been crushed. Pour into a glass and top with the lime slice.

YIELD: 1 SERVING

Appetizers

Appetizers are my favorite part of any restaurant menu. I think you really can judge a restaurant by how good the appetizers are. Often this is where the most creativity happens. For me, I'd usually be happy with a cocktail and a couple of appetizers.

I love to make appetizers at home, too. Sure, I love going out to eat, but ordering an appetizer, entrée, dessert, and maybe a drink—it really adds up. So here is a collection of carefully selected appetizers for you to enjoy. We have fruit salsas, jalapeño poppers with shrimp, quesadillas, and much more.

CopyKat.com's CHACHO'S™

Mango Salsa

One time some friends and I dared to order Chacho's really big plate of nachos. Our nachos filled a large pizza pan, and the four of us couldn't consume even half of them. Chacho's has a salsa bar, and their mango salsa is a favorite of many. Now you can enjoy this delicious fresh salsa for your next nacho adventure.

1 cup diced jicama

1 cup diced red onion

2 cups seeded and chopped tomatoes

1 cup chopped fresh mango

1 or 2 jalapeño peppers, seeded and finely chopped

½ cup chopped fresh cilantro

2 teaspoons freshly squeezed lemon juice

1 teaspoon salt

Combine all the ingredients in a medium bowl and stir well. This salsa will stays fresh for 3 to 4 days, stored in an airtight container in the refrigerator. I like to put it on top of grilled fish or grilled chicken to add flair to a meal.

YIELD: APPROXIMATELY 3 CUPS

NOTE: If you remove the seeds from the jalapeño peppers you'll remove most of the heat, so choose the heat level you want by removing the seeds or leaving them in. And keep in mind that not all jalapeño peppers are created equal, so you may want taste one of yours to see just how hot it is before you proceed.

Santa Fe Dip

Cheddar's is a wonderful place to take your family. It isn't too expensive, and they have many tasty selections. One of my personal favorites is their Santa Fe Dip. My version of this spinach dip is made with three different types of cheese, and it is served with sour cream and salsa just like it is in the restaurant.

10 ounces frozen spinach, thawed and drained

½ cup finely diced white onions

1 (8-ounce) package cream cheese

½ cup shredded white Cheddar cheese

½ cup shredded Monterey Jack cheese

½ cup shredded mozzarella cheese

2 teaspoons minced garlic

½ teaspoon seasoned salt

½ cup sour cream

½ cup salsa

corn tortilla chips

Preheat the oven to 350°F. In a medium bowl, combine the spinach, onions, cream cheese, Cheddar cheese, Monterey Jack cheese, mozzarella cheese, garlic, and seasoned salt. Stir until well blended. Spread into a 1-quart casserole dish and bake for approximately 30 minutes, or until the top is nice and bubbly. Serve with the sour cream, salsa, and tortilla chips on the side.

YIELD: 4 SERVINGS

Texas Cheese Fries

Personally, I think Cheddar's best menu items are found in the appetizer list. These Texas Cheese Fries are simply loaded with bacon and cheese.

vegetable oil, for frying

1 pound frozen regular-cut French fries

8 ounces thin-sliced bacon, cut into small pieces

6 ounces shredded Cheddar Jack cheese mix

ranch dressing, for serving

Preheat the oven to 425°F. Pour about 3 inches of oil into a deep saucepan. Heat the oil to 350°F. Cook the fries according to the package directions. If you are using a small deep fryer, fry them in small batches so all the fries get golden and crisp. Drain the fries on a cooling rack to keep them nice and crisp.

Cook the bacon in a skillet over medium heat until brown and crispy. Drain on paper towels. Pile the cooked French fries onto an ovenproof plate, leaving a well in the middle (for placing a small container of ranch dressing). Add the shredded cheese and bacon pieces. Place in the hot oven for 7 to 8 minutes, or until the cheese just begins to brown. Remove from the oven, place a small bowl of ranch dressing in the center of the plate, and serve.

YIELD: 4 SERVINGS

CopyKat.com's H-E-B®

Blue Cheese Ball

If you live in Texas, you know about H-E-B. This is a grocery store chain that I personally love. Why? Low prices, and some of the best product selection that you could find in a grocery store. Want special condiments from England, your favorite brand of rice from the Middle East, and other specialty items galore? They also make many things in-house, and their deli always offers something creative, like this cheese ball. I really like that it is made with simple ingredients and not a lot of fillers and additives. Cheese balls always signaled the holiday season in my house growing up, but they used to come in bright orange colors and tasted only sort of like cheese. This recipe is made from cream cheese and wonderful Danish blue cheese.

1 (8-ounce) package cream cheese, softened

⅓ cup crumbled Danish blue cheese

½ cup sliced almonds or chopped walnuts

In a medium bowl, combine the cream cheese and blue cheese. Stir together well. Cover and refrigerate overnight; the cream cheese will become firm again. Roll the mixture in a sheet of parchment or waxed paper to shape it into a ball. Place the nuts in a bowl and press the cheese ball firmly into them, turning it to coat all sides.

YIELD: 1 CHEESE BALL, ABOUT 8 SERVINGS

Grilled Artichokes and Garlic Aioli

For this recipe I have to thank Fran Feldman of the fabulous blog Thinrecipes.com. Jackson's is a restaurant in the Washington, D.C., area that's known for its tasty artichokes.

1 artichoke	3 garlic cloves, minced
1 lemon, cut in half	salt and pepper to taste
¼ cup water	2 tablespoons olive oil, if using a grill pan
¼ cup good-quality mayonnaise	

Trim the artichoke—cut off the stem and clip the spiny tips of the leaves. Squeeze half of the lemon onto the cut portions to prevent discoloration. Turn the artichoke upside down, placing the stem-side up (for stability) in a microwave-safe bowl and add the water. Cover with a lid or plastic wrap and microwave for 7 to 8 minutes. Take care not to overcook it, or the leaves may become soggy. Larger artichokes may need an additional 2 to 3 minutes in the microwave. Remove from the microwave and shock by running the artichoke under cold water to stop the cooking process. When cool enough to handle, cut in half lengthwise and carefully remove the prickly choke.

In the meantime, make the aioli in a separate bowl by combining the mayonnaise, 2 teaspoons lemon juice (from the remaining lemon half), garlic, and salt and pepper; mix until well combined. Let sit for at least 15 minutes to marry the flavors before serving.

Grill the artichokes in the kitchen with a stovetop grill pan or outside on a grill. If using a grill pan, pour 2 tablespoons olive oil into the pan. Place the artichokes on the pan, cut-side up, and grill over medium heat for 5 to 7 minutes, then flip over and grill the cut side for an additional 5 to 7 minutes. Season with salt and pepper as desired. Serve with the garlic aioli.

YIELD: 2 SERVINGS

CopyKat.com's **KROGER**®

Jarlsberg Dip

Jarlsberg is a fine cheese, rich and nutty; this recipe turns this it into a wonderful cheese spread. This dip is sold in Kroger stores, but you can make it at home. My favorite way to enjoy it is to spread it on rye bread and place it under the broiler until the cheese begins to melt and brown.

4 ounces freshly grated Jarlsberg or Swiss cheese

2 tablespoons mayonnaise

1 tablespoon finely chopped red onion

crackers, for serving

Combine the cheese, mayonnaise, and onion in a medium bowl and blend well. Cover and refrigerate for at least 2 hours to let the flavors mingle. Serve with crackers. This will stay fresh in the refrigerator, covered, for about a week.

YIELD: 4 SERVINGS

Grilled Chicken Flatbread

This flatbread is perfect as an appetizer or as party food. You can put it together in no time. You can purchase flatbread at the grocery store, and while the Olive Garden doesn't use naan, I think it also works well in this recipe.

1 cup Alfredo sauce (recipe on page 97)

1 tablespoon vegetable oil

1 boneless, skinless chicken breast

salt and pepper

1 garlic clove

1 (8-ounce) package flatbread

½ to 1 grilled red pepper, depending on your personal preference and the pepper size (see sidebar)

¼ cup shredded mozzarella cheese

¼ cup chopped fresh basil

Prepare the Alfredo sauce according to the recipe on page 97. Warm the vegetable oil in a skillet over medium-low heat. Season the chicken breast with salt and pepper and place in the skillet. Cook for about 4 minutes on one side, flip over, and cook on the other side for 3 to 4 minutes. Slice the chicken into thin diagonal slices.

Preheat the oven to 350°F. Cut the garlic clove in half and rub the cut side over the flatbread. Arrange the cooked chicken slices on the flatbread, coat the bread with Alfredo sauce, covering the bread and the chicken, top with half of the grilled red peppers, and sprinkle the mozzarella cheese on top of everything. Place the bread on a baking sheet and then place in the oven until the cheese melts, about 6 to 8 minutes. Remove from the oven and top with the remaining grilled red peppers and the chopped basil.

YIELD 4 SERVINGS

HOW TO GRILL PEPPERS

IN THE OVEN: Preheat the broiler. Lightly coat the pepper with olive oil and place on a baking sheet. Grill under the broiler until the skin turns black and the pepper softens slightly. Depending upon your oven, this may take as little as 3 or 4 minutes, or it could take as long as 10 minutes. Your guide to the cooking time will be the darkening of the pepper's skin. Rotate the pepper as it browns on each side. Place in a paper bag with plenty of space for the pepper, and let cool for about 20 minutes, then peel off the blackened skin.

ON A GAS STOVETOP: Turn your burner flame on high. Using metal tongs, place the pepper directly on the burner; flip over once one side is blackened, and continue to flip the pepper until it has been blackened on all sides. Place in a paper bag with plenty of space for the pepper and let cool for about 20 minutes, then peel off the blackened skin.

Fried Mushrooms

Logan's Roadhouse is a wonderful sit-down casual place that serves what tastes like some of the best home-cooked food you've tried. I love their environment—it's fun. You can walk in and enjoy roasted peanuts, and you get to throw the shells on the floor. The only problem is that there are so many good things to try. I love their fried mushrooms. Fresh white button mushrooms are carefully fried and served with a delicious horseradish dipping sauce (see the following recipe).

vegetable oil, for frying

1 pound fresh button mushrooms

2 cups all-purpose flour

2 teaspoons salt

1½ teaspoons ground black pepper

1 cup buttermilk

½ cup water

Pour oil into a large saucepan or deep fryer to a depth of 3 to 4 inches. Heat the oil to 350°F. Gently clean the mushrooms with a damp paper towel. If the stems are very large, trim them off; if the mushrooms are young and small, there is no need to trim them. Combine the flour with the salt and pepper in a bowl. Combine the buttermilk and water in another bowl.

Dredge the mushrooms in the seasoned flour, shaking off the excess, and then dip them in the buttermilk. Dredge in the flour a second time, shake off the excess, and carefully lower them into the hot oil. The mushrooms will take about 2 to 3 minutes to cook; they will be golden brown and begin to float when they're done. Drain on a wire cooling rack set over a baking sheet. (Using a rack instead of paper towels lets the grease drain away and keeps the crust from steaming off.) Serve with Horseradish Dipping Sauce (page 31).

YIELD: 4 SERVINGS

Horseradish Dipping Sauce

This inspired recipe can be used as a dip for Logan's Fried Mushrooms (previous recipe), but it also works well as a sandwich spread or even with your favorite steak or roast. There's something about this creamy horseradish sauce that makes everything you dunk in it taste better.

½ cup sour cream

3 tablespoons light mayonnaise

3 tablespoons prepared horseradish

1 teaspoon seasoned rice wine vinegar

¼ teaspoon salt

⅛ teaspoon onion powder

In a small bowl, whisk all the ingredients together. For best flavor, allow the flavors to mingle for about 1 hour before serving. Store the sauce in the refrigerator in an airtight container. This sauce will lose its heat within a few days, so be sure to consume it quickly.

YIELD: APPROXIMATELY ¾ CUP

CopyKat.com's **LOGAN'S ROADHOUSE®**

Loaded Potato Skins

I love making potato skins, because they are relatively easy and you can freeze them or prepare them many hours ahead and then cook them just before serving.

3 medium russet potatoes (about 4 inches long)

2 tablespoons butter

6 ounces bacon (6 to 8 slices), diced into small pieces

½ cup shredded Cheddar cheese

½ cup Monterey Jack cheese

⅓ cup sour cream

Preheat the oven to 400°F. Prick the potatoes with a fork in a couple of places. Bake for approximately 1 hour. As soon as the potatoes have cooled enough to handle, cut them in half lengthwise and carefully scoop out the center leaving approximately ¼ inch of flesh attached to the skin. Save the potato flesh that you scoop out—it will make wonderful hash browns, potato-and-egg breakfast tacos, or even mashed potatoes.

Turn the oven to broil. Melt the butter and brush it onto the potato flesh. Place the potato skins on a baking sheet and then place under the broiler for 8 to 10 minutes.

While the potatoes are under the broiler, cook the diced bacon in a skillet over medium-low heat. When the bacon has crisped and browned, remove it from the skillet to drain on paper towels.

In a bowl, toss the cheeses together until they form a uniform mixture. Place about 1 tablespoon of cheese on each potato half and sprinkle on about 1 teaspoon of bacon. If there's leftover cheese or bacon, add it onto the potatoes. Place the potato skins back under the broiler until the cheese has melted and begins to bubble; this should only take 3 or 4 minutes. To serve, arrange the potato skins on a plate with a small bowl of sour cream in the center.

YIELD: 2 TO 3 SERVINGS

CopyKat.com's THE MELTING POT®

Wisconsin Trio Fondue

The Melting Pot is definitely a special occasion place. You eat most of your meal fondue-style, making for a wonderfully romantic dinner. To re-create their cheese fondue at home, you don't need a special fondue pot, but you can often find fondue pots at garage sales or secondhand stores. Or you can use a double boiler as a fondue pot, or make your own double boiler by filling a pot halfway with water and setting a heat-resistant bowl in it; bring the water to a low boil and make your fondue.

8 ounces butterkase cheese, shredded

8 ounces fontina cheese, shredded

¼ cup cornstarch (or you can use flour)

1 cup Chablis or other dry white wine

¼ cup dry sherry

1 tablespoon chopped shallots

1 teaspoon freshly ground pepper

4 tablespoons crumbled blue cheese

2 tablespoons chopped green onions

Granny Smith apple slices

raw broccoli florets

raw cauliflower pieces

baby-cut carrots

hearty bread cut into bite-size pieces

In a bowl, stir the butterkase and fontina cheeses and the cornstarch together so that the cheese is coated with the cornstarch; this is what will help the fondue thicken. In either a double boiler over simmering water or a fondue pot, heat the wine, sherry, and shallots together for a minute or two. Add approximately half the cheese mixture and whisk constantly until the cheese is melted. Add the remaining cheese mixture by handfuls, whisking until everything is incorporated. Finally, stir in the blue cheese and pepper.

Just before serving, top the melted cheese with the green onions. Offer the green apple slices, broccoli, cauliflower, carrots, and bread for dipping into the fondue.

YIELD: 2 TO 3 SERVINGS

Shrimp Fritta

If you haven't had the chance to try the Olive Garden Shrimp Fritta, you are missing out on crispy fried shrimp surrounded by a buttery lemon wine sauce. I think this is one of the best shrimp appetizers out there. You could turn it into a main dish by simply mixing the sauce with cooked pasta and topping it with the shrimp.

vegetable oil, for frying

1 pound shelled, deveined shrimp

2 cups cornstarch

¼ cup dry white wine

1 cup unsalted butter, cut into tablespoon-size pieces and chilled

¼ cup white wine vinegar

2 tablespoons finely chopped onion

⅓ cup heavy cream

¼ teaspoon salt

⅛ teaspoon white pepper, or to taste

5 or 6 lemon slices

½ teaspoon fresh parsley

1 tablespoon freshly squeezed lemon juice

Fill a large pan with 3 to 4 inches vegetable oil. Heat the oil to 350°F. Dredge the shrimp in the cornstarch, shake off the excess, and fry the shrimp in small batches for 2 to 3 minutes, or until golden brown. Drain on a wire rack until ready to use.

In a heavy-bottomed skillet, heat together the wine, butter, vinegar, and chopped onion over medium heat until the liquid is reduced to 2 tablespoons; this should take about 10 minutes. Stir in the cream, salt, pepper, lemon slices, parsley, and lemon juice. Stir to combine. Place the cooked shrimp on a serving plate and drizzle with the wine sauce.

YIELD: 4 SERVINGS

Spinach and Artichoke Dip

What makes the Outback Steakhouse Spinach Artichoke Dip different from other restaurants? I think it's the amount of artichokes in the dip. Artichokes are more expensive than spinach, and some places don't add enough of them. I use frozen artichoke hearts for this recipe, so it really has a nice and clean flavor. Enjoy the dip with your favorite pita bread or crackers.

10 ounces frozen artichoke hearts, thawed

6 ounces frozen spinach, thawed and squeezed to remove the excess moisture

3 tablespoons chopped onion

1 cup cream cheese (8 ounces)

1 cup shredded Monterey Jack cheese

¼ cup grated Romano cheese

1 cup grated Parmesan cheese

½ teaspoon seasoned salt

Preheat the oven to 350°F. Chop the artichoke hearts into bite-size pieces. In a large bowl, combine the artichoke pieces with the spinach, onion, cream cheese, Jack cheese, Romano cheese, Parmesan cheese, and seasoned salt. Stir until well blended. Spread the mixture into a pie plate and bake for 25 to 30 minutes, or until the cheese is nice and bubbly.

YIELD: 8 TO 10 SERVINGS

Alice Springs Quesadillas®

Who doesn't love a quesadilla? These are so easy to prepare, and best of all, this is a great way to turn leftover bacon or grilled chicken into something new. I find that when you reinvent leftovers, finicky eaters will eat this meal without complaint.

2 tablespoons mayonnaise

1 tablespoon prepared yellow mustard

2 teaspoons honey

4 ounces grilled chicken breast

2 teaspoons butter, plus ½ teaspoon for the grill (or use nonstick spray)

2 ounces sliced baby portabella mushrooms

½ teaspoon garlic salt

¼ teaspoon chopped fresh parsley, plus more for optional garnish

4 (10-inch) flour tortillas

3 ounces shredded Colby-Jack cheese mix

4 slices bacon, cooked crisp

Prepare the honey mustard by combining the mayonnaise, mustard, and honey in a small bowl. Mix well and set aside. Slice the chicken breast on the diagonal into short slices about ¼ inch thick; set aside.

Use nonstick spray or about ½ teaspoon butter to coat the surface of a skillet or grill. If using a grill, heat it to approximately 350°F. Sauté the mushrooms over medium-high heat in a skillet with the 2 teaspoons butter, garlic salt, and parsley. Cook the mushrooms quickly—you want them to brown on the outside. They will take about 2 minutes to cook. Transfer to a bowl.

Sprinkle half the cheese on a tortilla. Add half the mushrooms, chicken, and bacon. Top with another tortilla. Cook for 2 to 3 minutes in the same skillet that the mushrooms were cooked in, flip very carefully, and cook for another 2 to 3 minutes. Repeat with the remaining 2 tortillas.

Use a pizza cutter to cut each quesadilla into quarters. Serve with the honey mustard sauce. To add flair, sprinkle a little fresh parsley on the finished dish, if desired.

YIELD: 2 SERVINGS

CopyKat.com's **PEI WEI ASIAN DINER®**

Crab Rangoon

Not all Crab Rangoon is made equal. Some comes with hardly any crab in it at all. It's no fun having to send out a search party for part of your dinner. Pei Wei Asian Diner is known for its high quality, and its food is served generously.

⅔ cup cream cheese, softened to room temperature

1⅓ cups crabmeat (about 10 ounces)

½ teaspoon soy sauce

2 teaspoons diced scallion

2 teaspoons diced red bell pepper

1 teaspoon lemon juice

¼ teaspoon ground white pepper

vegetable oil, for frying

1 (12-ounce) package wonton wrappers

sweet chili sauce, for serving

In a medium bowl, mix together the cream cheese, crabmeat, soy sauce, scallion, red pepper, lemon juice, and white pepper. Stir to combine well.

Pour enough oil into a small pot to cover the bottom 3 to 4 inches; heat to 350°F.

Fill a small bowl with water and dot the edges of a wonton wrapper with water. Place about 1 teaspoon crab filling in the center of the wrapper. Bring the diagonal edges of a wonton together, pinch them shut, and bring the other two edges together and close the edges as well. If the edges don't stay shut, add a little water and pinch them closed again. Fry in the hot oil in small batches until golden brown, 2 to 3 minutes. Drain on a wire rack. Serve with sweet chili sauce.

YIELD: 36 TO 40 PIECES

TIP: Chili sauce can be found in the Asian section of most grocery stores. Trader Joe's Sweet Chili Sauce is highly recommended.

Lettuce Wraps

These lettuce wraps make a wonderfully seasoned chicken appetizer—and are relatively lower in calories than many appetizers. This recipe calls for Maggi seasoning, which is similar to soy sauce but a bit different in flavor. If you have never purchased it before, you will find it useful in making soups, stocks, and gravies. For a milder dish, remove the seeds from the jalapeño.

1 tablespoon soy sauce

1 teaspoon seasoned rice wine vinegar

1 tablespoon sugar

1 teaspoon Maggi seasoning

2 tablespoons freshly squeezed lime juice

1 teaspoon chili garlic sauce

1 tablespoon sesame oil

2 tablespoons vegetable oil

2 teaspoons finely minced garlic

1 pound ground chicken breast

4 ounces fresh white button mushrooms, diced

1 large jalapeño pepper, diced

¼ cup chopped fresh basil

lettuce leaves (butter lettuce and iceberg lettuce both work well)

In a small bowl, combine the soy sauce, vinegar, sugar, Maggi seasoning, lime juice, and chili garlic sauce. Heat a wok over high heat and add the sesame and vegetable oils to the wok. Toss the garlic quickly in the hot oil and then add the chicken and mushrooms over medium-high heat. When the chicken is almost cooked through, add the jalapeño and basil. When the chicken has cooked completely, pour the sauce over it.

Transfer the chicken mixture to a platter and arrange lettuce leaves around the edges. To prepare the lettuce leaves, remove a whole leaf from the head of lettuce, wash, and pat dry with a paper towel. To eat, spoon some of the chicken mixture into each the lettuce leaf. Grasp the lettuce leaves to hold in the meat mixture and eat like a taco.

YIELD: 4 SERVINGS

CopyKat.com's **Red Lobster®**

Buffalo Chicken Bites

The Red Lobster does many dishes well, including their very spicy and crispy buffalo chicken bites. They serve theirs up a little differently than many other restaurants. The bite-sized spicy chicken bites have blue cheese crumbled on the top for a rich, flavorful topping.

4 cups vegetable oil, for frying

¾ cup all-purpose flour

1 tablespoon rice flour

½ teaspoon salt

¼ teaspoon ground black pepper

½ cup buttermilk

¼ cup water

1 (8-ounce) chicken breast

¾ cup Frank's Red Hot Sauce

6 tablespoons butter, melted

2 cups sliced Romaine lettuce (⅜-inch pieces)

1 tablespoon blue cheese crumbles

1 teaspoon minced fresh parsley

Preheat the oil to 350°F in either a deep fryer or a medium pot on the stove. In a small bowl, combine the flours, salt, and pepper; whisk to blend well. In another bowl, combine the buttermilk and water.

Cut the chicken into bite-size pieces. Dredge the chicken pieces in the seasoned flour mixture, dip into the buttermilk and water mixture, and then dredge again in the seasoned flours. Be sure to shake off all the excess flour. Fry the chicken in the hot oil until golden and crispy, 4 to 5 minutes. Drain on paper towels.

Arrange the lettuce on a serving plate. In a small saucepan heat together the hot sauce and butter. Stir to combine as the butter melts. Remove from the stove and dip the chicken bites in the warm buffalo sauce. Place the sauced chicken on top of the lettuce, top with blue cheese crumbles and fresh parsley, and serve immediately.

YIELD: 4 APPETIZER SERVINGS

CopyKat.com's **RED LOBSTER®**

Shrimp Nachos

These nachos inspired by Red Lobster are made with light creamy cheese sauce and then topped with shrimp and all sorts of fresh vegetables. I love making these at home, where I can add as much shrimp as I like.

¼ to ½ pound raw peeled and deveined shrimp

¼ cup shredded Monterey Jack Cheese

1 cup shredded mild Cheddar cheese

4 ounces cream cheese

¼ cup milk, or more as needed

40 to 50 tortilla chips

2 plum tomatoes, diced

2 teaspoons chopped cilantro

1 tablespoon finely chopped red onion

1 teaspoon chopped fresh jalapeño pepper (or more, if you like your nachos spicy)

2 tablespoons sour cream

2 or 3 slices fresh jalapeño pepper, for garnish

Drop the shrimp into a medium pot of boiling water. (I personally like to add a little crab boil seasoning to the water to give the shrimp an additional layer of flavor, but this isn't necessary.) Cook the shrimp until they turn pink; this will only take 2 to 4 minutes. Remove from the boiling water immediately. Stop the shrimp from cooking by immersing in cold water.

Prepare the cheese sauce by combining the Jack, Cheddar, and cream cheeses in a medium pot over low to medium heat. Stir in the milk to thin the sauce; you can add additional milk if you desire.

Preheat the oven to 350°F. Place the tortilla chips on a large ovenproof plate. Heat the chips until they are crisp, 5 to 7 minutes. While the chips are heating, prepare the pico de gallo by stirring together the tomatoes, cilantro, onion, and chopped jalapeño.

Assemble the nachos by spooning cheese sauce over the chips. Then top with the pico de gallo and the shrimp. Garnish your nachos with sour cream and slices of fresh jalapeño.

YIELD: 2 MAIN DISH OR 4 APPETIZER SERVINGS

Boiled Shrimp and Avocado Salsa

Hands down, this has to be one of my favorite appetizers to make at home. It's simple to prepare, and you can make your own modifications according to your personal preferences. If you like ceviche, you will also like this appetizer. This tangy salsa is packed full of tomato, onion, cilantro, avocado, lime juice, and freshly boiled shrimp. Personally, I like to add extra cooked shrimp and avocado.

¼ pound medium, raw shrimp, peeled and deveined

3 cups chopped tomatoes

⅔ cup finely chopped red onion

½ cup finely chopped sweet yellow onion

⅔ cup Heinz Chili Sauce*

⅔ cup coarsely chopped fresh cilantro

2 tablespoons freshly squeezed lime juice

2 teaspoons (or more) finely diced jalapeño pepper

1 avocado, diced

1 teaspoon salt

tortilla chips, for serving

* Heinz chili sauce is sold in most grocery stores, near the cocktail sauce or ketchup.

Bring a small pot of water to boil. Cook the shrimp in the water just until they turn pink, 2 to 3 minutes. Remove the shrimp from the boiling water and immerse in cold water to stop the cooking process. Chop half of the shrimp into small pieces.

In a medium bowl, stir together the tomatoes, red and yellow onions, chili sauce, cilantro, lime juice, jalapeño, avocado, and salt. Add the chopped shrimp. You can place the remaining shrimp on top for decoration, or you can simply stir it into the salsa. Serve with chips.

YIELD: 4 SERVINGS

Lemon Pepper Zucchini

Zucchini is carefully battered and deep fried, then lightly dusted with lemon pepper for this appetizer. Ideally, you should select zucchini that are straight and uniform in shape.

canola oil, for frying

2 (10-inch) zucchini

1 cup all-purpose flour

¼ cup cornstarch

1 teaspoon salt, plus more for sprinkling

1 cup whole milk

1 egg

1 teaspoon lemon pepper

buttermilk dressing, for dipping

Pour oil into a saucepan or deep fryer to a depth of 3 to 4 inches and heat to 350°F.

Prepare the zucchini by slicing off both ends, then cutting in half crosswise and cutting the halves lengthwise into quarters; you should end up with 8 spears from each zucchini.

In a small bowl, blend together the flour, cornstarch, and salt. In another small bowl, whisk together the milk and egg. Dredge the zucchini spears in the flour mixture, then the milk mixture, and then again in the flour. Shake off excess flour and drop the pieces into the hot oil. Fry for 3 to 4 minutes. The zucchini will be golden brown and float in the oil when they are done. Drain on paper towels. Sprinkle with lemon pepper and salt, and serve with your favorite buttermilk dressing for dipping.

YIELD: 2 TO 3 APPETIZER SERVINGS

CopyKat.com's SALTGRASS STEAKHOUSE®

Range Rattlers™

This recipe must have had its inspiration in the Gulf Coast of Texas. Here, jalapeño poppers are stuffed with shrimp and Monterey Jack cheese to make a for a unique jalapeño popper. Many jalapeño popper recipes do not ask you to steam the jalapeños first. I really feel that if you take time to steam the pepper the finished result is a smooth heat instead of a raw pepper taste. Since the shrimp is delicate, I think it is necessary to take a moment to steam the pepper before serving.

8 large raw shrimp, peeled and deveined

8 medium to large jalapeño peppers

½ cup shredded Monterey Jack cheese

1 cup whole milk

1 egg

1 cup all-purpose flour

¼ teaspoon salt

½ teaspoon ground black pepper

1½ cup seasoned bread crumbs

vegetable oil, for frying

ranch salad dressing, for serving

Thread 1 shrimp onto each of 8 barbecue skewers, starting with the head and then gently easing on the shrimp body, straightening out the flesh.

Rinse the jalapeños, then set up a steamer and steam them. Place the skewers of shrimp in the steamer and steam until the shrimp turn pink, 2 to 3 minutes. Rinse the peppers under cool water so they aren't too hot to handle.

Remove the stem and cut a slit down the side of each pepper. Remove the seeds if you wish (if you like lots of heat, leave them in). Place 1 tablespoon shredded cheese and a steamed shrimp in each pepper, positioning the shrimp tail at the pepper's stem end.

In a small bowl, whisk together the milk and egg. In another bowl, stir together the flour, salt, and pepper. Place the bread crumbs in a third bowl. Dip each stuffed pepper into the milk mixture and then roll in the seasoned flour. Place on a wire rack and let dry for 5 to 10 minutes, then dip into the milk again and coat with the bread crumbs. Place on the rack again and let dry for 5 to 7 minutes. Dip into the bread crumbs a second time and let dry again. Allowing the coating to dry between layers will help keep it intact during frying.

Pour the oil into a large saucepan or deep fryer to a depth of 3 to 4 inches and heat to 350°F. Fry the stuffed and battered peppers in the hot oil for 2 to 3 minutes, or until golden brown. Remove from the oil and drain on a metal rack.

Serve with ranch dressing for dipping.

YIELD: 4 SERVINGS

Mozzarella Cheese Sticks

Sonic has so many delicious menu items. One of the best, I think, is their cheese sticks, served with either marina sauce or ranch dressing. Yes, you can fry cheese sticks at home—it isn't difficult, and you can save yourself some money. If you use a mixture of all-purpose and rice flours, you'll notice a difference in the browning and crispness of the fried cheese sticks. Rice flour can be purchased in small amounts.

vegetable oil, for frying

1 cup all-purpose flour (or ¾ cup flour and ¼ cup rice flour)

½ teaspoon seasoned salt

2 cups Italian-seasoned bread crumbs

2 eggs

¼ cup water

1 pound mozzarella cheese

ranch dressing or marina sauce, for serving

Add enough oil to a deep skillet or deep fryer to fill the bottom 2 or 3 inches. Heat the oil to 350°F. In a bowl, whisk together the flour and seasoned salt. Place the bread crumbs in another bowl. In another bowl, whisk together the eggs and water.

To prepare the cheese sticks, cut the mozzarella into 32 sticks. Dredge the sticks in the flour, dip into the egg mixture, and then dredge in the bread crumbs. Be sure to coat the cheese as completely as you can. If you don't cover it completely, the melted cheese will leak out of the breading and quickly burn. Fry the cheese sticks, a couple at a time, for 30 seconds to 1 minute. Remove the cheese sticks from the oil and drain on a wire rack. Serve with your choice of marina or ranch dressing.

YIELD: 8 SERVINGS

TIP: You can also freeze the uncooked coated cheese sticks to fry later. Freeze them flat on a baking sheet, and then transfer the frozen cheese sticks to a zip-top bag. When frying these from a frozen state, they will take a few minutes longer to cook.

CopyKat.com's **STAR PIZZA™**

Goat Cheese and Roasted Garlic

If you live in the Houston area, I'm certain you know about Star Pizza, a fantastic local restaurant that makes one delicious pizza. Among other menu items, one of the most creative is their goat cheese and roasted garlic appetizer. The flavors of the fresh goat cheese and the roasted garlic, served with fresh bread, mingle so well together in this easy-to-prepare appetizer.

2 garlic bulbs

2 to 4 teaspoons olive oil

1 loaf fresh bread (baguettes and Italian bread work well)

3 to 4 ounces goat cheese

1 tablespoon sun-dried tomato slivers

1 tablespoon chopped fresh parsley

Preheat the oven to 400°F. Peel away the loose skin covering the garlic, but leave enough skin so the bulb stays intact. Cut about ¼ or ⅜ inch off the top of the garlic; this should expose most of the individual cloves. Drizzle each garlic head with enough olive oil to coat the top. You may want to spread the oil around with your fingers; if you don't cover the cloves with oil, they may burn. Wrap each garlic bulb in foil and place them on a baking sheet. Bake for approximately 30 minutes. You'll know the garlic is done when it turns a golden color and is soft to the touch. Remove garlic from the oven and allow to cool while you plate the cheese and bread. When the garlic is cool enough to handle, remove it from the foil.

Cut 6 to 8 slices of bread approximately ½ inch thick and arrange them on a plate. Place the goat cheese in a small dish in the center of the plate. Add the garlic bulbs to the plate. Sprinkle the sun-dried tomatoes and chopped parsley over the plate. To enjoy this appetizer, spread a little goat cheese on a piece of bread and top with a peeled roasted garlic clove.

YIELD: 2 TO 4 APPETIZER SERVINGS

CopyKat.com's **SPAGHETTI WAREHOUSE®**

Classic Bruschetta

Spaghetti Warehouse is a fun, family-friendly Italian restaurant chain with old-time décor that includes a trolley car in each location. The food is reminiscent of good, old-fashioned cooking, and the prices are reasonable. This stuffed bruschetta makes a lovely appetizer or a nice light lunch.

½ baguette

1 small bunch fresh basil

2 or 3 Roma tomatoes

1 pound fresh mozzarella cheese, thinly sliced

2 tablespoons balsamic vinegar reduction (recipe on page 188)

Cut the baguette into ⅜-inch slices. To toast the bread, heat your oven broiler on high, place the baguette slices on a baking sheet, and broil just until the bread begins to turn brown. Remove the baking sheet from the oven and flip the slices over, then brown on the other side.

Slice the basil into tiny strips by rolling several leaves together and cutting very thin. Thinly slice the tomatoes.

To assemble each bruschetta, top a piece of toasted bread with a thin slice of mozzarella and then a thin slice of tomato. Sprinkle on basil and drizzle with balsamic vinegar reduction.

YIELD: 4 SERVINGS

Sausage and Mozzarella Bruschetta

Like an appetizer that's a little hearty? This bruschetta is topped with Italian sausage, tomatoes, and a little balsamic vinegar reduction. If you buy a 1-pound package of sausage, you can easily use what's left over in spaghetti sauce for an easy dinner.

8 ounces Italian sausage links	pinch of salt
½ baguette	1 pound fresh mozzarella cheese, thinly sliced
3 or 4 basil leaves	
1 Roma tomato, chopped	2 tablespoons balsamic vinegar reduction (recipe on page 188)
1 teaspoon olive oil	

Preheat the oven to 350°F. On a broiler pan, or a wire cooling rack placed on a baking sheet, bake the sausage for approximately 30 minutes, or until done. Let cool and then cut into diagonal slices approximately ¼ inch think.

Slice the baguette into ⅜-inch slices. To toast the bread, heat your oven broiler on high, place the baguette slices on a baking sheet, and broil just until the bread begins to turn brown. Remove the baking sheet from the oven and flip the slices over, then brown on the other side.

Slice the basil into tiny strips by rolling several leaves together and cutting them very thin. In a small bowl, stir together the chopped tomato, basil, olive oil, and salt.

Preheat the oven to 250°F. To assemble the bruschetta, place a thin slice of mozzarella on each bread slice and top with sausage. Place in the warm oven for 3 to 4 minutes, or just until the cheese begins to melt. To serve, top with the tomato mixture and drizzle with balsamic vinegar reduction.

YIELD: 4 SERVINGS

CopyKat.coms's **T.G.I. FRIDAY'S®**

Classic Mediterranean Hummus

One of the reasons I love T.G.I. Friday's is that they make their food right there. I know, you'd think all restaurants would prepare 100 percent of their food on the premises, but they don't. Here the food is hand-crafted in the restaurant, and the flavor comes through. I love this hummus, to which they add a traditional bruschetta mixture of fresh tomatoes, garlic, and basil. Topped with creamy yogurt, a thin slice of jalapeño, green onions, and Sriracha sauce, it's served with grilled pita bread.

HUMMUS:

1 (15-ounce) can chickpeas, rinsed and drained

¼ cup plain yogurt

1 teaspoon minced garlic

½ teaspoon kosher salt

2 teaspoons olive oil

2 tablespoons freshly squeezed lemon juice

¼ teaspoon ground cumin

1 tablespoon tahini

BRUSCHETTA TOPPING:

1 cup chopped Roma tomatoes (about 3 tomatoes)

1 tablespoon chopped fresh basil

½ teaspoon kosher salt

1 teaspoon minced garlic

2 tablespoons olive oil

FOR SERVING:

4 or 5 pieces of pita bread

nonstick cooking spray

2 tablespoons plain yogurt

1 thinly sliced jalapeño pepper

Sriracha sauce

1 tablespoon sliced green onion

TO MAKE THE HUMMUS: Use a food processor to combine the beans, yogurt, garlic, salt, olive oil, lemon juice, cumin, and tahini. Pulse until smooth and creamy.

TO MAKE THE BRUSCHETTA TOPPING: Combining the chopped tomatoes, basil, salt, garlic, and olive oil. Stir until just blended. (This will taste best if you can make it an hour or two ahead of time.)

FOR SERVING: To toast the pita bread, heat a griddle to medium-high heat. Spray the bread with a little nonstick spray and lay it on the hot griddle. You want to toast the pita just until brown marks appear. If you don't have a griddle, you can heat the bread in a hot skillet until it begins to brown. Cut the warm bread into triangles.

To assemble, scoop the hummus into a bowl and top with several spoonsful of the tomato mixture. The extra bruschetta mix can be served alongside, or refrigerated and used later. Add the 2 tablespoons yogurt in a nice dollop. Garnish with thinly sliced jalapeño—many slices if you like lots of heat, 2 or 3 slices if you like less heat. Shake on Sriracha sauce to taste, and top with the green onions. Serve along with the pita triangles for dipping.

YIELD: 4 SERVINGS

CopyKat.coms's **T.G.I. FRIDAY'S®**

Pretzel Sticks and Beer Cheese

Who doesn't love going to T.G.I. Friday's? They are known for delicious drinks and some of the most inventive food around. Their Pretzel Sticks and Beer Cheese is the perfect appetizer for watching the big game.

PRETZEL STICKS:

2¼ teaspoons or 1 package instant yeast

1 cup plus 2 tablespoons warm water (125 to 130°F)

2 tablespoons plus 1 teaspoon sugar, divided

4½ cups to 5 cups of all-purpose flour, plus more for rolling

1 teaspoon salt

vegetable oil, for bowl

8 cups water

¼ cup baking soda

1 egg white lightly beaten with 1 teaspoon water, for glaze

1 tablespoon coarse kosher salt, for sprinkling

BEER CHEESE SAUCE:

8 ounces American cheese*

4 to 6 ounces beer

American cheese can be purchased in bulk from the deli counter at your grocery store. They can cut a large chunk of the cheese. This cheese is also great to make nacho cheese sauce for tortilla chips.

TO MAKE THE PRETZEL STICKS: Proof the yeast by combining it with 2 tablespoons warm water and 1 teaspoon sugar in a small bowl. Once the yeast begins to foam and bubble, it is ready to use. Transfer the yeast mixture to the bowl of a stand mixer and add the flour and salt; begin to mix, using the dough hook. Slowly stream the remaining 1 cup warm water into the flour; a ball of dough will form. Continue to mix for another minute to knead the bread.

Grease a bowl with vegetable oil, place the dough ball in the bowl, cover with a towel, and let rise for approximately 35 minutes. The dough should double in size.

Flour a cutting board and place the dough on the board. Knead and then divide the dough into 12 portions. Roll each portion into a small cigar shape and use a sharp knife to cut 2 or 3 slits into the top. Cover with a towel and let rise for another 25 minutes.

Preheat the oven to 375°F.

On the stovetop, bring the 8 cups water to boil in large saucepan. Add the baking soda and the remaining 2 tablespoons sugar (the water will foam up). Drop 4 pretzel sticks at a time into the boiling water and cook for 30 seconds per side. Use a slotted spoon to remove the sticks and place them on the prepared baking sheet.

Brush the pretzels with the egg white glaze and sprinkle generously with coarse salt. Bake until brown, about 25 minutes. Transfer to wire racks and let cool for 10 minutes. Serve warm or at room temperature.

TO MAKE THE BEER SAUCE: Chop the cheese into small pieces and place in a small saucepan. Pour in the beer and heat over low heat until the cheese has melted, stirring with a whisk to combine.

Transfer the cheese sauce to a small bowl and serve with the pretzels for dunking.

YIELD: 4 SERVINGS

Soups

Soups can be a light meal or something you turn to when you need a little homestyle comfort. In this chapter, I will show you how you can make some favorite restaurant soups in your own kitchen. Many of these soups reheat very well, so you can enjoy them the second day—which makes them perfect to bring with you to work. Taking your lunch to work a couple times a week can be a great money saver.

I'll show you how to make a broccoli cheese soup that's just as rich and creamy as the one at Panera Bread. I'll also share with you how to make the Olive Garden's chicken gnocchi soup—one of the Internet's most saved recipes as measured by ZipList's recipe saving program. Soon you'll be making your own tomato and basil soup just like the one at La Madeleine. So whip out your favorite soup pot, and let's get started.

CopyKat.coms' APPLEBEE'S®

French Onion Soup

One of my favorite soups to have when eating out is French onion. There's something about the taste of caramelized onions that is so good. A heavy dose of melted cheese makes this soup irresistible. Applebee's often uses hamburger buns for their bread, but I find a heartier bread holds up better for this soup.

2 tablespoons butter

2 tablespoons vegetable oil

10 cups sliced onions (6 or 7 large onions)

1 teaspoon salt, plus more to taste as desired

1½ teaspoons chopped garlic

10 cups low-sodium beef broth

1 tablespoon beef base*

1 teaspoon ground black pepper

8 thick slices firm bread

8 teaspoons grated Parmesan cheese

8 tablespoons shredded provolone cheese

* Beef base is a paste that flavors soups much like bouillon cubes but adds more flavor and less salt. You'll find it near the soups in the grocery store.

In a large stockpot over medium heat, first heat the butter and oil, then add the sliced onions and salt; sauté the onions until they are browned. This will take up to 30 minutes; you want the onions to have the color of caramels. Stir frequently to prevent burning.

When the onions are almost fully caramelized, add the chopped garlic. Cook the onions and garlic together until the garlic has become fragrant, about 2 mintues. Add the beef broth, beef base, and black pepper. Taste and add more salt if needed. Simmer for 30 to 45 minutes over low heat.

To serve the soup, preheat the oven to broil. Ladle soup into 8 individual ovenproof bowls, place a bread slice on top of each, and top each slice with 1 tablespoon of each cheese. Place under the broiler on a baking sheet until the cheese begins to brown.

YIELD: 8 SERVINGS

CopyKat.coms' LE CELLIER STEAKHOUSE™

Canadian Beer Cheese Soup

Le Cellier Steakhouse is found in Disney's Epcot in Florida, in the Canada Pavilion. Don't try to make this soup if you're in a hurry—you need to let the cheese melt gently, and rushing won't give you good results. I recommend using Tillamook brand cheese if you can get it. America's Test Kitchen recommends it, and I agree that it's a tasty cheese. Don't try to save time by buying shredded cheese. An anticaking agent is used to keep the cheese from sticking together in the package, and it may not melt well.

I would serve this soup with some lovely hearty dark beer.

1 (12-ounce) bottle good-quality dark beer*

½ pound applewood-smoked bacon, sliced into small pieces

¼ cup (½ stick) butter

1 cup chopped red onion

1 cup thinly sliced celery

1 cup flour

3 cups low-sodium chicken broth

2 cups heavy cream

1 pound shredded aged white Cheddar cheese

1 tablespoon Tabasco sauce

1 teaspoon ground white pepper

1 teaspoon dry mustard powder

1 tablespoon Worcestershire sauce

* Brands/styles of beer that I like include Shiner Bock, Saint Arnold's Amber, Abita Beer Amber, and any Oktoberfest-style of beer.

Open the bottle of beer and set it on the counter to warm up if it has been refrigerated.

Heat the bacon in a large stewpot over low heat. Don't try to brown it; you just want to release the fat. When a couple tablespoons of fat have been released and the bacon begins to look cooked, add the butter. When the butter has melted, turn heat up to low-medium and add the chopped onion and celery. When the onion begins to look translucent and the celery is tender, stir in the flour. This will look crumbly, and it may appear that you have too much flour. Cook for a couple of minutes, stirring, so the raw flour taste is cooked out.

Add 1 cup of the chicken stock, stirring until the mixture is thickened and looks like gravy. Add the rest of the chicken stock a cup at a time, stirring to incorporate each time. The mixture will look like a thick gravy now. Add half the cream, stir until incorporated, and then stir in the remaining cream. Add the shredded cheese a third at a time, stirring until all the cheese is fully melted. Add the Tabasco, pepper, dry mustard, and Worcestershire, and stir until fully blended. Slowly pour in the beer, stirring until well blended. Serve the soup immediately.

YIELD: 10 TO 12 SERVINGS

TIP: If you must reheat this soup, do so very gently over low heat on the stovetop. You may need to thin the soup with a little milk.

CopyKat.com's **KROGER®**

Bread Bowls

You've seen these fancy bread soup bowls in many of your favorite restaurants, and you've seen them at some grocery stores. Purchasing one or two bread bowls isn't too expensive, but if you want to serve them to your whole family it can be a costly proposition. Even if you aren't an experienced bread maker, though, you can make great-tasting bread bowls at home. This recipe uses mostly regular flour and a bit of semolina for flavor and texture. If you don't have semolina, you can omit it and use about 2 teaspoons less water.

1½ cup warm water	1 teaspoon salt
2¼ teaspoons or 1 package instant yeast	vegetable oil, for bowl
1 tablespoon sugar	vegetable shortening, for baking sheet
3 cups all-purpose flour	cornmeal, for dusting
2 tablespoons semolina flour	

Combine the warm water in a bowl with the yeast and sugar. The yeast will be ready to use in a couple of minutes, when it bubbles and begins to foam. Add the yeast mixture to the flours and salt in a mixing bowl. Use either a stand mixer with dough hook or blend and then knead by hand until the dough is soft and smooth. Place the dough in a bowl with about 1 teaspoon oil, and turn the dough to coat with oil on all Allow the dough to rise in a warm place, covered, for 1 to 1½ hours or until the dough has doubled in size.

Grease a baking sheet and lightly dust with cornmeal. Divide the dough into 5 or 6 portions. Form into balls and place on the prepared baking sheet. Cover and allow the dough to rise again until the dough balls have doubled in size, about 1 to 1½ hours.

Uncover the balls and let them sit for 10 to 15 minutes, to develop a tough skin. Preheat the oven to 425°F.

Before baking, sprinkle or mist the bread bowls with water. Bake for about 20 minutes, or until a deep, golden brown. Remove from the oven and let cool completely before cutting the tops off the bread bowls and scooping out the insides. If you're going to use the bread bowls later, let them cool completely before wrapping them. Serve with your favorite soup.

YIELD: 5 OR 6 BREAD BOWLS

TIP: I like to proof my yeast before using it in a recipe. That way I know that it's still active. If you purchase a package of yeast and use it before the expiration date, you don't need to follow this step. I often buy yeast in bulk because it's cheaper that way. I store it in my freezer, so it is generally past the expiration date by the time I use it.

CopyKat.com's **LA MADELEINE™**

Tomato Basil Soup

La Madeleine is a wonderful French bistro and bakery. They are known for their delicious Caesar salads, soups, and much more. I love that you can go there and get a delightful bakery treat or a hot meal. This version of their tomato soup is so easy to make that you can have it ready in just 20 minutes or so.

2 (14½-ounce) cans crushed or diced tomatoes

2 cups tomato juice

2 cups chicken broth

12 to 14 fresh basil leaves, divided

1 cup heavy cream

¼ cup (½ stick) butter

salt

¼ teaspoon cracked black pepper

In a medium saucepan over medium-low heat, combine the tomatoes, tomato juice, chicken broth, and half of the basil. Simmer for 30 minutes. Purée with an immersion blender, or pour into a blender in small batches and purée until the tomatoes are mostly smooth. Return to the saucepan over low heat and add the cream and butter, stirring, until the butter is melted. Season with salt and pepper. Garnish with the remaining basil leaves and serve.

YIELD: 4 SERVINGS

CopyKat.com's **OLIVE GARDEN®**

Chicken Gnocchi Soup

This is the most popular recipe at CopyKat.com. I really recommend using leftover chicken if you can, especially the rotisserie type available at many grocery stores. Rotisserie chicken has a lot of flavor and really makes the soup taste great.

1 tablespoon extra-virgin olive oil

¼ cup (½ stick) butter

¼ cup flour

½ cup finely diced celery

1 cup finely diced onion

2 garlic cloves, minced

4 cups half-and-half

1 (12-ounce) package gnocchi*

1 cup finely shredded carrots

1 cup diced cooked chicken breast

2 (14-ounce) cans chicken broth (if you enjoy thick soup, use just 1 can)

1 cup coarsely chopped fresh spinach

½ teaspoon salt, plus more if needed

½ teaspoon dried thyme

½ teaspoon dried parsley

¼ teaspoon grated nutmeg (optional)

You can find dried gnocchi in the pasta section of most grocery stores; some stores also sell fresh or frozen gnocchi. You may want to cut your gnocchi in half before cooking if it is large, or purchase the mini size if available.

Heat the olive oil and butter in a large saucepan over medium heat. Add the onion, celery, and garlic and sauté until the onion becomes translucent. Whisk in the flour to make a roux. Let the flour mixture cook for about a minute and then stir in the half-and-half.

Cook the gnocchi according to the package directions. Drain and set aside.

Meanwhile, add the carrots and chicken to the roux. Once the mixture has thickened, stir in the chicken broth. When the mixture thickens again, add the cooked gnocchi, spinach, and seasonings; simmer the soup over medium-low heat until it is heated through. Taste and adjust the seasoning with more salt if needed.

YIELD: 8 SERVINGS

CopyKat.com's **OLIVE GARDEN®**

Pasta e Fagioli

This is one of the Olive Garden's best-known soups.

2 tablespoons vegetable oil

1 pound ground beef

1 cup chopped yellow onion

1 cup shredded carrots

1 cup diced celery

3 (14-ounce) cans beef broth

2 (14-ounce) cans diced tomatoes

2 (24-ounce) jars marinara sauce

1½ teaspoons dried oregano

1½ teaspoons ground black pepper

1½ to 2 teaspoons salt

1 teaspoon Tabasco sauce

1 tablespoon chopped fresh parsley

1 (14-ounce) can red kidney beans, drained and rinsed

1 (14-ounce) can white beans, drained and rinsed ·

4 ounces dried ditallni pasta*

If you don't have ditalini pasta—"little thimbles"—you can substitute another small pasta. Small shells and small penne both work well.

Heat the vegetable oil in a large pot over medium heat. Sauté the beef in the oil until it begins to turn brown and then add the onions, carrots, and celery. When the onions become translucent, pour in the beef stock, scraping the bottom of the pan to lift up the browned bits. Add the tomatoes, marinara sauce, oregano, pepper, salt, oregano, and Tabasco; simmer for about 10 minutes. Stir in the chopped parsley and beans and simmer on low heat for about 45 minutes, until all the vegetables are soft.

In a separate a pot, cook the pasta according to the package directions; drain. Add the pasta to the soup just before serving to keep it from overcooking and becoming mushy.

YIELD: 10 TO 12 SERVINGS

TIP: If you want to prepare this soup in a slow cooker, first brown your meat in a skillet. Then place all the ingredients except the pasta in a 6-quart slow cooker, cover, and cook on low for approximately 6 hours. Just before serving, cook the pasta according to the package directions and add it to the slow cooker.

Baked Potato Soup

The Outback Steakhouse is known for their delicious steak, coconut shrimp, and Aussie fries, to name just a few dishes. But did you know they have a wonderful baked potato soup? The Outback does something a little different to their soup, baking their potatoes first and adding them to the soup last thing. This makes for nice, firm pieces of potato.

- 4 medium russet potatoes
- 1½ cup chopped white onion
- ½ cup (1 stick) butter
- ½ cup plus 2 tablespoons all-purpose flour
- 4 cups low-sodium chicken broth
- 4 cups heavy cream

- 1 teaspoon salt, or to taste
- 1½ teaspoons ground black pepper, or to taste
- 8 slices bacon, fried until crispy and crumbled
- ½ cup shredded Cheddar cheese
- ¼ cup chopped green onion

Preheat the oven to 400°F. Bake the potatoes for approximately 1 hour. When they are easily pierced by a fork, remove the potatoes from the oven and let them cool until they are easy to handle. Peel and chop into bite-size cubes; set aside.

In a large pot over medium-high heat, cook the chopped onions in the butter until they are translucent. When the onions are clear, add all the flour. Stir for 1 to 2 minutes to cook out the raw flour taste. You'll know it's ready when the flour begins to smell like cooked pie crust.

Stir in 1 cup of the chicken broth; the mixture should thicken rapidly. Once it has thickened, add another cup of broth. When the mixture thickens again, add the remaining 2 cups broth. Stir in 2 cups of the cream; allow the mixture to thicken slightly, and then add the rest of the cream. Let the mixture come to a soft boil and then reduce the heat to low. Add the diced potato, salt, and pepper. Taste and adjust the seasonings as needed.

To serve, top each bowlful of soup with bacon, cheese, and chopped green onions.

YIELD: 8 TO 10 SERVINGS

CopyKat.com's **PANERA BREAD®**

Broccoli Cheese Soup

For some people, this may be the only way they knowingly eat broccoli. This creamy and cheesy soup isn't hard to prepare at home. If you're feeling extra fancy, you may want to purchase ready-made bread bowls from your grocery store's bakery department and serve your soup in them just as Panera Bread does. (Or you can make your own bread bowls—see page 57.)

- 2 tablespoons butter
- 2 tablespoons all-purpose flour
- ½ cup chopped yellow or white onion
- 1 cup half-and-half
- 1 (16-ounce) package frozen chopped broccoli, thawed and drained

- 1 (1-pound) loaf processed cheese food (Velveeta or a store brand), cubed
- 2 (14½-ounce) cans low-sodium chicken broth
- 1 cup julienne-cut carrots (or shredded carrots)
- 8 ounces Cheddar cheese, shredded
- salt and pepper

In a large saucepan over medium-high heat, heat together the butter, flour, and chopped onion. Cook, stirring, for about a minute, then pour in about a quarter of the half-and-half and whisk until thickened and smooth. Slowly add the rest of the half-and-half the same way.

When the half-and-half has been incorporated, add the broccoli and processed cheese. When the cheese is melted, stir in the chicken broth a cup at a time until the soup is well mixed and has a consistent texture. Add the carrots and simmer for about 20 minutes. During the last 10 minutes, stir in the shredded Cheddar cheese. When all the cheese is completely melted, season to taste with salt and pepper, and serve.

YIELD: 6 TO 8 SERVINGS

CopyKat.com's PANERA BREAD®

Creamy Tomato Soup

As an adult, I finally learned the magic of tomato soup and grilled cheese sandwiches. Soup out of the can isn't exactly the most appetizing, and you can prepare a wonderful creamy tomato soup from scratch. Canned tomatoes are used here because they are always in season, and I find that they are very predictable in terms of water content and great to use in cooked recipes.

¼ cup (½ stick) butter

½ cup chopped onion

½ teaspoon chopped garlic

4 tablespoons flour

2 cups half-and-half

1 teaspoon sugar

½ teaspoon baking soda

1 teaspoon salt

1 teaspoon ground black pepper

¼ teaspoon red pepper flakes

½ teaspoon dried oregano

3 (14½-ounce) cans diced tomatoes

½ teaspoon Italian seasoning

In a large pot over medium-high heat, melt the butter and add the chopped onion and garlic. Cook until the onion becomes translucent, stirring occasionally so the garlic doesn't brown. Add the flour and cook for 1 to 2 minutes, stirring continually to keep the flour from browning. Add 1 cup of the half-and-half and stir until the mixture thickens, then add the remaining 1 cup half-and-half. When the soup base has thickened, stir in the sugar, baking soda, sugar, salt, pepper, red pepper flakes, oregano, tomatoes, and Italian seasoning.

Use an immersion blender or transfer the soup to a standard blender to purée it until it is almost smooth—but be sure to leave some small pieces in the soup. Simmer the soup over low heat for about 15 to 20 minutes for the flavors to mingle before serving.

YIELD: 4 SERVINGS

Creamy Herbed Turkey Soup

This soup is only served during December at Sweet Tomatoes. This is a great way to use leftover turkey, but you could make the soup with chicken. While Sweet Tomatoes makes its own stuffing, I think you can use the stovetop kind and have a wonderful bowl of soup.

4 cups water

1 cup diced carrots

1 cup diced celery

½ cup (1 stick) butter

1½ cups chopped onions

¾ cup flour

6 cups turkey broth

2 teaspoons poultry seasoning

1 cup cooked turkey meat

1 teaspoon salt

1 teaspoon ground black pepper

1 tablespoon chopped flat-leaf parsley

2 cups heavy cream

1 (6-ounce) box instant turkey stuffing, prepared according to package directions

In a medium pot over medium-high heat, combine the water, celery, and carrots. Cook for 10 to 12 minutes, until the vegetables are tender. Drain and set aside.

Start the soup by making a roux: Melt the butter in a large stockpot over medium heat. Add the onions to the melted butter and cook until transparent. Then add the flour and reduce the heat to medium-low and cook for 1 to 2 minutes, stirring. The color should darken and the roux should smell like cooked pie crust. Turn the heat up to medium and add 1 cup turkey broth to the mixture. Stir until thickened. Add another cup of turkey stock, and stir again until thickened. You may need to raise the heat just slightly to ensure rapid thickening. Add 2 cups more broth, stir until thickened, and then add the remaining 2 cups broth.

Add the turkey meat, cooked celery and carrots, poultry seasoning, salt, pepper, and parsley. Stir until well mixed. Add the heavy cream and cook for an additional 10 to 15 minutes over medium-low heat. Cook the stuffing according to the package directions. To serve, ladle soup into bowls and top with the cooked stuffing.

YIELD: 8 TO 10 SERVINGS

Roasted Mushroom Soup with Sage

Sweet Tomatoes is a wonderful place to go for fresh soups and salads. Also known as the Soup Plantation, the restaurant makes soups from scratch every day. Since they have so many different kinds of soups, you have to catch it just right to get your favorite—or you can make your own version at home.

- 12 ounces white button mushrooms, sliced
- 4 ounces cremini mushrooms, sliced
- 2 tablespoons vegetable oil
- ¼ cup (½ stick) butter
- ½ cup chopped onion
- ¼ cup flour
- 2 cups heavy cream
- 2 cups milk
- ½ teaspoon dried sage
- 1 teaspoon salt

Preheat the oven to 350°F. Spread the sliced mushrooms on a rimmed baking sheet and drizzle the vegetable oil over them. Lightly salt the mushrooms and bake for approximately 30 minutes.

In a large saucepan over medium-high heat, melt the butter and sauté the chopped onions. Cook, stirring occasionally, until the onions become translucent, then stir in the flour and reduce the heat to medium. Cook for 1 to 2 minutes, stirring. Turn the heat up to medium-high, add 1 cup of the cream, and stir until the mixture has thickened. Add the remaining 1 cup of cream; once this has thickened, add the milk. Stir in the baked mushrooms and the sage. Use an immersion blender, or transfer the soup to a blender and purée it for a few moments. Season with salt before serving.

YIELD: 6 TO 8 SERVINGS

TIP: This soup can also be made with all heavy cream. If you want to reheat your soup later, cream reheats better than the mixture of milk and cream. You can also use all white button mushrooms; just use 16 ounces total. However, combining the two kinds of mushrooms gives a more intense mushroom flavor.

Main Dishes

Main dishes are what drive us out of our homes and into our favorite restaurants, whether it be for pasta, pizza, or a great salad. I think that one of the reasons so many of us love making copycat recipes is that we get to alter these dishes to suit our personal taste. On the following pages you'll find recipes for hearty chicken salads, pizzas, chicken Alfredo, and much more.

Grilled Chicken and Pecan Salad Sandwich

If you've never had one of these fruit-infused chicken sandwiches, you're missing out on a unique way to prepare chicken salad. Packed full of grilled chicken breast meat, grapes, apples, and pecans, this hard-to-beat chicken salad is served on toasted bread.

1 cup diced red-skinned apple

1 tablespoon freshly squeezed lemon juice

2½ cups diced grilled chicken breast

1 cup sliced red grapes

½ cup chopped celery

1 cup chopped pecans

½ to ¾ cup mayonnaise

salt and pepper

8 thick slices toasted wheat bread

green leaf lettuce leaves

In a medium bowl, mix the diced apple and lemon juice, stirring to coat the apples with the juice. (This will help keep the apples from turning brown.) Add the chicken, grapes, celery, and pecans. Mix well until everything is thoroughly combined. Stir in ½ cup mayonnaise; if the mixture seems too dry, you can add another ¼ cup mayonnaise. Add salt and pepper to taste. Refrigerate, covered, for about 1 hour to allow the flavors to marry.

To prepare a sandwich like Arby's, line a thick slice of wheat bread with a couple of lettuce pieces, spread on about 1 cup of chicken salad, and top with another slice of bread.

YIELD: 4 SANDWICHES

TIP: While Arby's doesn't toast their pecans, I think you could easily bring this salad to the next level by toasting the nuts in a skillet over medium high-heat just until they become fragrant. Allow the pecans to cool completely before preparing the chicken salad.

CopyKat.com's ALONTI'S™

Pesto Pasta

Alonti's is a restaurant that's often located in large office complexes. We've all had pesto made with basil, garlic, olive oil, and pine nuts, but Alonti's does a twist on traditional pesto. They use pecans instead of pine nuts, adding a dimension that is simply delicious.

25 fresh basil leaves

½ cup extra-virgin olive oil

4 or 5 garlic cloves

1 teaspoon kosher salt

½ cup pecans

1 cup grated Parmesan cheese

2 tablespoons grated Romano cheese

1 pound dried pasta

Wash the basil leaves and place in the bowl of a food processor along with the olive oil and garlic. Pulse several times, until the garlic begins to break into small pieces. Add the salt and pecans and process briefly at medium speed, then add the cheeses and pulse until they are mixed uniformly through the pesto.

Cook the pasta according to the package directions. Pour the pesto over the cooked pasta, mix well, and serve. If you don't intend to eat all of the pesto at once, refrigerate the remaining pesto in an airtight container; it will remain fresh for a couple of days.

YIELD: 4 SERVINGS

Bourbon Chicken

This recipe is meant to emulate a flavor found in many malls across America. I've never seen any of those places actually add any bourbon to their chicken. Here is my version, complete with bourbon. You may want to serve this with rice, because the sauce is so tasty you won't want to miss a single drop.

2 tablespoons canola oil or seasoned stir-fry oil

1 teaspoon minced garlic

1 teaspoon minced fresh ginger

2 tablespoons minced onion

1 pound chicken leg or thigh meat, cut into bite-size pieces

½ cup bourbon whiskey

⅓ cup water

2 teaspoons rice wine vinegar

1 tablespoon ketchup

⅓ cup soy sauce

1 teaspoon chili garlic sauce

1 teaspoon cornstarch (optional)

Heat a wok to high and add the oil. Whisk the oil around in the wok, add the garlic and ginger, and quickly stir so they don't burn. Add the onion and chicken and stir-fry until the chicken is cooked through.

In a small bowl, combine the bourbon, water, rice vinegar, ketchup, soy sauce, and chili garlic sauce. If you want a thickened sauce, mix in the 1 teaspoon cornstarch. Pour the sauce into the wok, stirring to coat the chicken. Transfer the mixture to a serving dish.

YIELD: 4 SERVINGS

CopyKat.com's **CARRABBA'S ITALIAN GRILL®**

Chicken Bryan

Carrabba's is an Italian restaurant where you can watch the cooks prepare your food, thanks to their open-kitchen concept. This dish features grilled chicken with a lemon butter sauce, topped with goat cheese.

4 boneless, skinless chicken breasts	2 teaspoons chopped garlic
salt and pepper	¾ cup dry white wine
olive oil for brushing	2 tablespoons freshly squeezed lemon juice
8 ounces goat cheese	
½ cup (1 stick) cold butter, divided	2 tablespoons thinly sliced fresh basil, divided
¼ cup chopped white onion	2 tablespoons sliced sun-dried tomatoes

Wrap each piece of chicken in plastic wrap and pounding until thin, about ⅜-inch thick. Remove the plastic wrap and pat the chicken dry with a paper towel. Season with salt and pepper and brush with olive oil. Cook the chicken on a grill until cook through, 3 to 4 minutes on each side. Place the cooked chicken on a plate and cover lightly with plastic wrap. Slice the goat cheese into 4 slices and shape into disks, one for each piece of chicken.

To prepare the sauce, heat 2 tablespoons of the butter in a saucepan over medium heat, then sauté the onions and garlic in the butter. Cook until the onions and garlic are fragrant and the onions are translucent. Add the wine and lemon juice to pan and simmer gently until the wine has been reduced by half. Then add 3 tablespoons of cold butter and whisk until it has melted completely; turn off the burner, add the remaining 3 tablespoons butter, and whisk it in. The sauce should be getting thick now. Pour the sauce through a strainer to strain out the onions and garlic, then return the strained sauce to the warm pan and stir in half the basil and all the sun-dried tomatoes.

To serve, place the chicken breasts on individual serving plates, top with the goat cheese, and spoon the sauce over the chicken. Sprinkle on the remaining basil.

YIELD: 4 SERVINGS

Broccoli Cheddar Chicken

This recipe idea came from a gentleman gave me a call and told me this was his favorite dish from the Cracker Barrel. Once he called, I went to the restaurant to try the dish. But the Cracker Barrel has a seasonal menu, and by the time I got there, this item was gone. A year or so later, I went in, saw the dish on the menu, and tried it. I quickly went to work on this recipe, and here is the result: a carefully cooked chicken breast topped with buttery Ritz crackers, broccoli, and cheese.

1 (10.5-ounce) can Campbell's Cheddar Cheese Soup

1 soup can milk (measure in empty cheddar cheese soup can)

4 boneless, skinless chicken breasts

½ teaspoon seasoned salt

8 ounces frozen broccoli, thawed

¼ cup (½ stick) butter, melted (you can use more)

1½ cups Ritz cracker crumbs

4 ounces shredded Cheddar cheese

Preheat the oven to 350°F and spray a baking dish with cooking spray. Mix the cheese soup according to the directions on the can (1 can of soup to 1 can milk). Place the chicken breasts in the prepared baking dish and sprinkle with the seasoned salt. Pour ¾ of the prepared soup over the chicken. Scatter the broccoli over the soup-covered chicken.

In a bowl, combine the melted butter with the cracker crumbs. Sprinkle the mixture over the broccoli, add the remaining soup, and bake for approximately 45 minutes, or until the chicken is cooked through. (Cut into the thickest part of the chicken and check to see that the meat is uniform in color.) Remove from the oven and sprinkle with the shredded cheese.

YIELDS: 4 SERVINGS

CopyKat.com's CRACKER BARREL OLD COUNTRY STORE®

Sunday Chicken

The name says it all—this recipe is really only available on Sunday. If you are lucky enough to be around the restaurant then, you can enjoy this perfectly fried chicken breast. If you aren't so lucky, well, here's my version. The chicken breasts are prepared just like your grandmother made her fried chicken—dipped in seasoned flour, dunked in buttermilk, and dipped again in seasoned flour.

vegetable oil, for frying

4 boneless, skinless chicken breasts

2 cups all-purpose flour

2 teaspoons salt

2 teaspoons ground black pepper

1 cup buttermilk

½ cup water

Pour 3 to 4 inches of oil into a deep fryer or a large pot and preheat the oil to 350°F.

Prepare seasoned flour by combining the flour, salt, and pepper in bowl. Stir to combine well. In another bowl, mix together the buttermilk and water. If your chicken breasts are not fairly uniform in size, place them between pieces of plastic wrap and use a meat pounder to gently pound the breasts into more uniform pieces about ⅜ inch thick. Pat dry with a paper towel.

Season the chicken breasts with a little salt and pepper. Dredge them in the seasoned flour, dip in the buttermilk, and then dredge again in the seasoned flour. Shake off the excess flour and deep-fry the chicken pieces in the hot oil for 7 to 8 minutes, or until golden brown, turning halfway through. Drain the chicken on a wire rack.

YIELD: 4 SERVINGS

CopyKat.com's **DAIRY QUEEN®**

Dude

Years ago, and I mean years ago, I put myself through college by working in restaurants. Dairy Queen was one of my first jobs. I loved this chicken-fried steak sandwich. When we ran out of the frozen ones we often used, we had to batter up our own. While we used to batter frozen hamburgers for this recipe, I think beef cutlets make a nice change.

vegetable oil, for frying

4 (4-ounce) tenderized beef cutlets (you can use top sirloin, cube steak, or round steak)

2 cups all-purpose flour

1 teaspoon salt, plus more for sprinkling

½ teaspoon ground black pepper, plus more for sprinkling

1 cup buttermilk

½ cup water

4 hamburger buns

8 tomato slices

4 to 8 lettuce pieces

mayonnaise

Pour enough oil into a deep skillet to cover the bottom 1½ inches of the pan. Preheat the oil to 350°F.

In a shallow dish, use a fork to stir together the flour, 1 teaspoon salt, and ½ teaspoon pepper. In another shallow dish, mix together the buttermilk and water. Sprinkle the beef cutlets with salt and pepper. Dredge the meat in the seasoned flour, dip in the buttermilk, and dredge in the flour again. Ideally, allow the floured cutlets to rest for 10 to 15 minutes before cooking.

Fry the meat in the hot oil, flipping over when the bottom has browned. When both sides are browned, remove and let drain on paper towels.

Assemble each sandwich by placing a chicken-fried steak patty on the bottom bun, then adding tomato slices and then the lettuce. Spread mayonnaise on the top bun and place the bun on the sandwich.

YIELD: 4 SERVINGS

TIP: The restaurant serves these with mayonnaise, lettuce, and tomatoes, but I always loved to add onion, cheese, and pickle to my sandwich.

CopyKat.com's **DENNY'S**®

Club Sandwich

This recipe is here for sentimental reasons. This double-decker sandwich has always been one of my favorites. When I was a child, I felt like an adult with a club sandwich. Here we combine a bacon, lettuce, and tomato sandwich with a turkey sandwich. Some places swap out the turkey for ham, and you could do that. Personally, I love this classic taste. When you make this at home, you can always add more bacon if you wish. For a complete club sandwich experience, serve this with potato chips or French fries.

3 slices bread, toasted	2 slices bacon, cooked crisp
1 tablespoon mayonnaise	3 iceberg lettuce leaves
3 to 4 ounces sliced turkey	2 or 3 tomato slices

Lay out the toasted bread and spread the mayonnaise evenly on one side of each slice, leaving the other side dry. Arrange the turkey on the mayonnaise side of one slice of toast, then top it with another slice. Add bacon to the stacked bread, breaking it to fit the bread if necessary. Top with tomato slices, the lettuce leaves, and the remaining slice of bread, mayonnaise side down.

Insert 4 toothpicks into the sandwich, placing them in the center of each side about ½ inch from the crust. Cut the sandwich from corner to corner in both directions to make 4 triangles.

YIELD: 1 SANDWICH

Cordon Blue Sandwich

While this delightful sandwich may be on the value menu, it is one tasty chicken sandwich. This sandwich features fried chicken tenders, ham, and Swiss cheese, held together with honey mustard sauce. You can use already-frozen prepared chicken tenders, or you can make them from scratch yourself.

vegetable oil, for frying

1½ cups all-purpose flour

1 teaspoon salt

½ teaspoon ground black pepper

1 cup buttermilk

1 pound chicken tenders

2 to 3 tablespoons butter, softened

8 slices potato bread

8 slices processed Swiss cheese

8 ounces shaved or thinly sliced ham

Pour 2 to 3 inches of vegetable oil into a large pot and heat the oil to 350°F for frying. In a small dish, combine the flour, salt, and pepper, stirring well. Pour the buttermilk into another small dish. Dredge the chicken tenders in the seasoned flour, dip in the buttermilk, and then dredge in the flour again. Cook in the hot oil for 4 to 5 minutes, until browned, turning halfway through. Drain on a wire rack.

Prepare each sandwich by buttering one side of a slice of bread and placing buttered side down on a grill. Place 2 cheese slices on the bread, add the ham, and then add 2 chicken tenders. Drizzle honey mustard over the chicken. When the cheese has melted, top with the remaining piece of bread.

YIELD: 4 SANDWICHES

CopyKat.com's DENNY'S®

Fried Cheese Melt

Want an overboard sandwich for the cheese-lover you know? This is the one for you—a grilled cheese sandwich made with cheese sticks along with sliced cheese. While you can't enjoy one of these every day, this is a fun recipe to make and share.

2 slices sourdough bread

2 teaspoons butter, softened

4 slices American cheese (Kraft Deli Deluxe American slices are recommended)

3 frozen cheese sticks, prepared according to package directions

marinara sauce, for serving

Heat a skillet over low to medium heat. Butter one side of each bread slice and place 1 slice in the hot skillet, buttered side down. Cover with 2 cheese slices; you may need to break the slices apart to completely cover the bread. Lay the cooked cheese sticks on top, spaced equally. Add the remaining cheese slices and top with the remaining slice of bread, buttered side up. Cook on both sides until the bread is golden brown and the cheese is melted. Serve with marina sauce.

YIELD: 1 SANDWICH

CopyKat.com's **DOUBLE DAVE'S PIZZAWORKS®**

Thanksgiving Pizza

Double Dave's is known for unique and creative pizzas. They put together flavors that you never would have thought of before. This Thanksgiving pizza is a great way to use leftovers from holiday meals. It features turkey, gravy, stuffing, and yes, even cranberry sauce. If you don't have turkey gravy, you can substitute chicken gravy.

1 pound pizza dough

1 cup turkey gravy

2 tablespoons chopped onions

¾ cup prepared stuffing (if you don't have leftovers, you can use StoveTop Chicken Flavor)

½ to 1 cup chopped cooked turkey

2 tablespoons jellied cranberry sauce

1 cup shredded mozzarella cheese

Preheat the oven to 425°F. Spay a 24-inch pizza pan with nonstick spray. Roll out the pizza dough right in the pan. Ladle on the gravy and sprinkle the onions over the gravy. Add the stuffing and turkey, and top with the cheese.

Bake for 15 to 17 minutes, or until the cheese is golden brown. Remove from the oven and add the cranberry sauce in small portions over the pizza top.

YIELD: 3 TO 4 SERVINGS

CopyKat.com's **JAMES CONEY ISLAND**™

Frito Pie

You can order a Frito Pie at James Coney Island as a side dish or even as a main dish. If you've never had a Frito Pie, it's a wonderful crunchy treat. You may want to dress up your "pie" with some diced onion or a little shredded cheese.

¼ cup vegetable oil

2½ pounds chuck steak, diced finely

2 (10½-ounce) cans beef broth

3 cans water (use the broth can)

2 (14.5-ounce) cans whole tomatoes with their juices

1 tablespoon paprika

5 teaspoons chili powder

1 teaspoon garlic powder

1 teaspoon onion powder

¾ teaspoon seasoned salt

¼ teaspoon garlic salt

¼ teaspoon cayenne pepper

2 teaspoons cornstarch dissolved in ½ cup water

1 (16-ounce) bag Fritos corn chips

shredded cheddar cheese, for topping (optional)

chopped onions, for topping (optional)

In a 4-quart saucepan over medium heat, heat the vegetable oil. Brown the diced chuck steak in the hot oil, stirring frequently, until the meat is until lightly brown. Add the beef broth and water. Simmer for 1 hour over medium-low heat.

Meanwhile, process the tomatoes and their juices in a blender, then use a fine-mesh strainer to strain out the seeds and any pulp bits. Measure 2 cups of the strained tomatoes for the chili; save the rest for another use.

After the beef has simmered for 1 hour, add the 2 cups processed tomatoes and all the seasonings (paprika through cayenne pepper); stir well. Simmer for 45 to 50 minutes on low heat, stirring from time to time.

Slowly pour enough of the cornstartch mixture into the meat mixture to thicken it, stirring constantly. Depending on how much the liquid in the chili has been reduced, you may not need to use all of the thickener. Simmer over low heat, stirring, until the chili reaches the desired consistency.

Place corn chips in individual bowls, and then ladle chili over the Fritos. Cover most of the chips with chili; you can then top with shredded cheese and chopped onions, if desired.

<><><><><><><><><><><><><><><><><><>
YIELD: 12 SERVINGS

CopyKat.com's **JAMES CONEY ISLAND™**

Jucy Lucy

A friend once brought up one of my favorite hot dog places, James Coney Island, and mentioned how yummy their burger was. I had to try it out, and you know, I think they serve some of the best hamburgers around. My burger was grilled to order, the buns were toasted on the grill, the meat was perfectly cooked, and they even grilled the onions.

1½ pounds ground chuck

1 teaspoon salt

¾ teaspoon ground black pepper

4 slices cheese (American, Cheddar, or pepper Jack)

4 hamburger buns

1 tablespoon butter

½ cup chopped onions

2 teaspoons vegetable oil

4 teaspoons prepared mustard

12 dill pickle slices

4 teaspoons mayonnaise

Place the ground chuck in a bowl and mix in the salt and pepper. Form into 8 patties, ¼ inch thick. For each burger, cut a slice of cheese into quarters and arrange them to fit on a meat patty. Top with another patty and press the edges together so that no cheese will leak out while the burger is cooking.

Heat your grill to about 375°F. You can also use a skillet on medium heat. Place the patties on the grill and cook until the meat is browned on the bottom side. Do not press the patties, but leave them undisturbed while they cook. Flip and cook the other side for 3 to 4 minutes.

While the burgers are cooking, butter the hamburger buns and toast them on the grill, buttered side down, until golden brown. Sauté the onions in the vegetable oil until they are golden brown on the grill or in a skillet over medium heat, stirring frequently so they do not burn.

To assemble each burger, build up from the bottom. Spread 1 teaspoon mustard on the bottom bun, place 3 pickles over the bun. Add the grilled hamburger patty and top it with grilled onions. Spread mayonnaise on the top bun before placing it on top of the burger.

YIELD: 4 SERVINGS

CopyKat.com's **JOHNNY CARINO'S™**

Gorgonzola Chicken

The first time someone told me that Gorgonzola makes a tasty pasta sauce, quite frankly I thought they were nuts. But this is one of those recipes that people have requested over and over again, so I thought that maybe I should reconsider. I'm glad I did. Johnny Carino's typically uses penne pasta, but I like to use fettuccine because I think it holds the sauce better.

2 boneless, skinless chicken breasts	1 pound dry pasta*
salt and pepper	2 cups half-and-half
2 tablespoons vegetable oil	4 ounces crumbly Gorgonzola cheese
1 to 2 tablespoons butter, if needed	½ cup chopped red tomatoes
8 ounces white button mushrooms, sliced	2 tablespoons shredded Parmesan cheese

Pound the chicken breasts until they are uniformly ½ inch thick. Season with salt and pepper. Heat the vegetable oil in a skillet over medium-high heat and sear the chicken. Cook 4 to 5 minutes on each side, or until cooked through. Remove from the heat and let rest for several minutes.

If the skillet is dry, add 1 or 2 tablespoons of butter. Sauté the mushrooms over medium-high heat until browned. While they are cooking, sprinkle on about ½ teaspoon salt and stir frequently so they do not burn.

Cook the pasta according to the instructions on the package. Meanwhile, prepare the sauce by combining the half-and-half and the Gorgonzola in a saucepan and heating through over medium heat until slightly thickened. Stir in the sautéed mushrooms.

Cut the chicken into ¼-inch slices. To serve, divide the pasta between 2 plates and add the chicken slices. Drizzle with the sauce and top with chopped tomatoes and shredded Parmesan.

YIELD: 2 SERVINGS

CopyKat.com's **CAPTAIN D'S SEAFOOD RESTAURANT®**

Fried Fish

Growing up, I would frequently visit my grandparents in Jefferson City, Missouri. I was lucky to have both sets living there. Often on Friday nights they would go to Captain D's for fish. That was a long time ago, but if pressed I will tell you that this is still one of my fast-food vices. I love their fish. Honestly, I think they have food that's very comparable to dishes served at high-end restaurants.

4 cups vegetable oil for frying

1½ cups all-purpose flour

½ cup cornstarch

1 tablespoon baking powder

2 teaspoons kosher salt

½ teaspoon cayenne pepper

1½ cups water

4 fish fillets (cod, hake, or other mild white fish)

Preheat the oil to 350°F in either a deep fryer or a medium saucepan. In a medium bowl, mix together the flour, cornstarch, baking powder, salt, and cayenne pepper. Whisk in the water. The batter will get a little foamy; continue to mix.

Coat the fish in the batter, working to fully coat each fillet. Deep-fry for 3 to 4 minutes, or until golden brown. You may want to fry the fish a couple of pieces at a time, and you may need to separate the pieces while frying to keep them from sticking together. Drain on a wire rack.

YIELD: 4 SERVINGS

TIP: While recipe testing, I used club soda instead of plain water. If you have a SodaStream soda maker, you may want to give this a try. I don't think it's necessary, but I do think it gives the batter just a little more lift.

Bacon Cheddar Hamburger Steak

Luby's is a cafeteria that is well-known in Texas. Often, cafeterias prepare chopped beef steak that's served a little plain. Leave it to the folks at Luby's to dress up their hamburger steak with melted Cheddar cheese, crispy cooked bacon, and thinly sliced green onions.

2 pounds ground chuck

1 teaspoon seasoned salt

½ teaspoon ground black pepper

1 teaspoon Worcestershire sauce

1 (14.5-ounce) can beef broth

¾ cup shredded Cheddar cheese

¼ pound bacon, cooked crisp and chopped into small pieces

¼ cup thinly sliced green onions

In a bowl, combine the ground chuck with the seasoned salt, pepper, and Worcestershire sauce, mixing well. Shape into 6 oblong patties about ⅜-inch thick. Place the patties into a 9 x 13-inch baking dish. Cover the bottom of the dish with beef broth. Heat your oven's broiler on high. Broil the beef patties until completely done; this may only take 10 to 13 minutes. Top the cooked patties with cheese, bacon, and green onions and return them to the oven for about 1 to 2 minutes to allow the cheese to melt.

YIELD: 6 SERVINGS

CopyKat.com's **OLIVE GARDEN®**

Baked Pasta Romana

This baked pasta dish inspired by the Olive Garden uses lasagna noodles in a new way. Ideally you should make the recipe using leftover brisket or even roast. This is a great way to give leftover meat a spectacular second act.

2 tablespoons vegetable oil

1 onion, thinly sliced

salt and pepper

1 flat beef brisket, about 5 pounds

2 to 4 cups beef broth

2 tablespoons tomato paste

12 ounces dried lasagna noodles

1½ cups heavy cream

½ cup (1 stick) butter

½ cup grated Asiago cheese, plus more for garnish

½ cup shredded fontina cheese, plus more for garnish

¼ cup grated Parmesan cheese, plus more for garnish

½ cup fresh spinach

1 teaspoon olive oil

Preheat the oven to 350°F. In a Dutch oven over medium heat, heat the 2 tablespoons vegetable oil. Sauté the onions in the oil, sprinkling them with about ½ teaspoon salt. When the onions are translucent, transfer them to a bowl and set aside.

Sprinkle both sides of the brisket with salt and pepper. Place the meat in the Dutch oven and brown it on both sides, then transfer it to a plate. Pour 1 cup of beef broth into the pot, scraping the browned bits up from the bottom. Add the tomato paste and whisk together well. Return the onions and then the brisket to the pot; add enough broth to cover the brisket halfway. Bake, covered, for 3½ hours. The brisket is done when a fork slides into the meat easily. If the meat is still tough after the initial time, bake for an additional 30 minutes. Once the brisket is removed from the oven, let it rest for approximately 20 minutes before slicing.

Prepare the lasagna noodles as directed on the package. Once the drained noodles are cool enough to handle, cut them in half both vertically and horizontally. This way you won't get a whole lasagna noodle in a single bite.

For the sauce, combine the cream and butter in a saucepan over medium to medium-high heat. When the mixture just begins to simmer, whisk in ½ cup *each* of Asiago and fontina cheese and ¼ cup of Parmesan; the sauce will thicken. Remove the pan from the heat.

Spray a 2-quart casserole dish with cooking spray. Place the noodles in the dish, folding them over so they make nice curls. Pour the sauce over the noodles. Toss the spinach with the olive oil and arrange it around the sides of the casserole dish. Slice 6 to 8 ounces of beef and place it on the noodles; reserve the remaining brisket for other uses. You may want to spoon on a little of the cooking gravy from the brisket, too. Top with a little more of each cheese and place in the oven for 10 to 15 minutes, until the cheese melts on top of the pasta.

YIELD: 4 SERVINGS

TIP: You can make the brisket in advance, but I don't recommend making the pasta or the sauce ahead of time.

CopyKat.com's **OLIVE GARDEN®**

Grilled Chicken and Alfredo Sauce

One of my favorite menu items at the Olive Garden is the Alfredo sauce. If one recipe really got me started, it was this one. My big tip here is to grate your own cheese; prepackaged cheese has an anticaking agent on it, and it makes it harder to get that cheese to melt.

2 chicken breasts

salt and pepper

2 teaspoons olive oil

8 ounces dry pasta

2 cups heavy cream

½ cup (1 stick) butter

½ to ¾ cup grated Parmesan cheese (not preshredded or pregrated cheese)

1 teaspoon garlic powder

Preheat your grill to medium-high heat. Brush with olive oil and then season the chicken breasts with salt and pepper. Grill 5 to 7 minutes on the first side and then flip the chicken over and grill for another 3 to 4 minutes, or until cooled through. Cook the pasta according to the package directions.

Prepare the Alfredo sauce by combining the cream and butter in a saucepan over medium-high heat. Do not let the mixture come to a boil, but heat it until small bubbles begin to form. Add the Parmesan cheese and whisk quickly. Add the garlic powder and continue to whisk. The sauce will thicken after a minute or two.

Cut the chicken breasts into strips. Serve by placing half the pasta on each plate, then topping it with sauce and a sliced chicken breast.

(If you have extra sauce or pasta left over, it is best to store and reheat them separately so the pasta doesn't soak up the sauce.)

YIELD: 2 SERVINGS

Grilled Sausage Pepper Rustica

Did you know this menu item was brought back by the Olive Garden because of requests from people who loved it? I thought this alone was enough reason for me to re-create the recipe so that you could enjoy this sausage and penne pasta.

2 tablespoons olive oil, divided

1 pound Italian sausage links

2 bell peppers (red, green, yellow, or orange)

1 cup sliced onion (white or yellow)

½ teaspoon salt

¼ to ½ teaspoon red pepper flakes (optional)

1 (26-ounce) jar marinara sauce (I recommend Barilla Spicy Marinara)

1 pound dry penne pasta

½ cup shredded mozzarella cheese

In a large skillet over medium heat, heat 1 tablespoon of the olive oil. Slice the sausage into bite-size pieces and cook in the hot oil until browned. Remove the sausage from the pan and set aside. Add the remaining 1 tablespoon olive oil to the skillet. Add the sliced peppers and onions, season with the salt, and cook until the onions are translucent and the peppers are tender. Return the browned sausage to the pan and stir thoroughly. If you want your sauce to be spicy, add red pepper flakes to taste. Stir in the marinara sauce and heat well.

Cook the pasta according to the package directions. Add the mozzarella cheese to the sauce and stir until melted. Pour the sauce over the cooked pasta and toss well.

YIELD: 4 SERVINGS

CopyKat.com's **PANDA EXPRESS GOURMET CHINESE®**

Broccoli Beef

I'm suggesting a minor change from the way Panda Express serves this dish. I like to steam the broccoli a bit before adding it to the stir-fry to make sure it is completely done. You can use flank steak, sirloin, or even fillet. The trick here is to slice the beef nice and thin.

2 tablespoons oyster sauce	1 tablespoon cornstarch
2 tablespoons water	1 pound broccoli florets
2 tablespoons cooking wine, divided	2 tablespoons seasoned wok oil, or other high-heat oil (such as grapeseed) with a splash of sesame oil
1 tablespoon dark brown sugar	
1 tablespoon soy sauce	
1 pound flank steak (or sirloin or fillet)	2 teaspoons minced garlic
	1 teaspoon minced ginger

To make the sauce, in a small bowl, mix together the oyster sauce, water, 1 tablespoon of the cooking wine, brown sugar, and soy sauce.

Cut the flank steak into very thin slices and place in a bowl. To make the steak marinade, in a small bowl mix together the cornstarch and cooking wine and pour over the steak pieces. Marinate the meat for approximately 15 minutes.

While the steak is marinating, steam the broccoli in a steamer just until it turns bright green. Do not cook the broccoli all the way through—it will finish cooking when it is stir-fried.

Heat a wok or very large skillet over high heat; pour in the oil and swirl it around. Spread out the beef slices in the pan and let them cook on one side; discard the marinade. Turn the beef over after about 1 minute, add the garlic and ginger, and mix quickly. Add the broccoli and finishing sauce and stir everything together until the sauce has thickened.

YIELD: 4 SERVINGS

Firecracker Chicken Breast™

The Panda Express makes fresh small batches of many of your favorite Chinese recipes. This Firecracker Chicken is a wonderful light entrée, full of flavor but lower in calories than many dishes. The recipe includes an unusual ingredient, *douchi*—fermented black beans, available in Asian markets. If you can't find douchi, you can use black bean sauce instead.

⅓ cup soy sauce

1 teaspoon seasoned rice vinegar

1 teaspoon rice cooking wine

1 teaspoon sugar

1 teaspoon cornstarch

2 tablespoons seasoned wok oil or peanut oil

7 or 8 dried hot peppers

2 teaspoons chopped garlic

2 teaspoons chopped fresh ginger

1 cup sliced red bell pepper

1 cup sliced yellow bell pepper

1 cup sliced onion

1 pound skinless, boneless chicken breast, sliced thin

2 teaspoons douchi (fermented black beans) or 1½ teaspoons black bean sauce

In a small bowl, make the finishing sauce by combining the soy sauce, seasoned rice vinegar, rice cooking wine, sugar, and cornstarch. Stir until smooth and set aside.

Heat your wok over high heat until it begins to smoke. Add the seasoned wok oil or peanut oil. When the oil is hot, add the hot dried peppers and toss them for a moment or two before adding the garlic and ginger. Sauté briefly, add the sliced bell peppers and onion, and stir-fry until the onions are softened. Add the chicken and douchi and stir-fry until the chicken is browned. Pour in the finishing sauce and stir until the sauce has thickened.

YIELD: 4 SERVINGS

Honey Walnut Chicken

This recipe combines crispy fried shrimp and sweet crunchy walnuts. And while I love the Honey Walnut Chicken at the Panda Express, I also love to make this at home, where I can use larger and more walnut pieces and bigger shrimp. I have seen many recipes that have you prepare your own homemade tempura, but I've found that the packaged mix available in the Asian section of your grocery store produces better results. You really want a thick, crunchy shell on the shrimp to go with the creamy sauce.

1 cup walnut pieces	1 pound medium or large shrimp, peeled and deveined, tails removed
1 cup water	
¾ cup sugar	1 tablespoon honey
1 (10-ounce) package tempura mix	1 tablespoon sweetened condensed milk
vegetable oil, for frying	2 teaspoons lemon juice
	3 tablespoons mayonnaise

Place the walnuts in a saucepan with the water and sugar. Cook over medium to medium-high heat until the sugar begins to brown. Line a rimmed baking sheet with parchment paper or aluminum foil and pour the walnuts the paper or foil to dry for 20 to 25 minutes, spreading them out with a fork so they don't touch each other.

When the walnuts are almost dry, begin to prepare the tempura according to the package directions. Add enough oil to a pan to cover the bottom 2 to 3 inches; heat the oil to 350°F. Dip the shrimp in the tempura batter, covering them completely. Drop into the oil a few at a time and gently toss to make sure the shrimp cook evenly on all sides and don't stick together. Scoop out any batter that floats away from the shrimp to keep the oil from breaking down. Remove the shrimp after about 2 minutes and transfer to paper towels to drain.

To make the sauce, whisk together the honey, sweetened condensed milk, lemon juice, and mayonnaise. When all the shrimp is cooked, place it in a bowl and drizzle on the sauce. Stir to coat the shrimp, but be careful not to break off the crust. Sprinkle the candied walnuts over the shrimp and serve immediately. This recipe should be eaten in one sitting—it won't be as good if reheated.

∞∞

YIELD: 2 VERY LARGE SERVINGS OR 4 SMALL SERVINGS

TIP: I like to add about ¼ to ½ teaspoon red pepper flakes to the shrimp for a little heat.

CopyKat.com's **PEI WEI ASIAN DINER®**

Mongolian Beef

Pei Wei Asian Diner is very similar to P.F. Chang's, which owns Pei Wei, but Pei Wei has a more casual dining atmosphere and is a perfect place to grab a quick dinner or lunch. Here's my version of their Mongolian beef, made with flank steak and mushrooms and served in a dark, rich sauce.

8 ounces flank steak or skirt steak or beef tenderloin

¼ cup cornstarch

¼ cup vegetable oil

1 teaspoon sesame oil

½ teaspoon grated fresh ginger

2 garlic cloves, minced

⅓ cup soy sauce

⅓ cup water

1 teaspoon Maggi seasoning

½ cup packed dark brown sugar

1 teaspoon seasoned rice wine vinegar

4 ounces white button mushrooms, stems removed and quartered

2 or 3 green onions, green and white parts, chopped

Slice the beef very thin, approximately ¼ to ⅜ inches thick. If you are using skirt or flank steak, cut the meat diagonally to help make it more tender. Place the meat between sheets of plastic wrap and use a meat tenderizer to gently pound it into uniform pieces; the meat should be ¼ inch thick. Place the cornstarch in a shallow bowl. Dip the steak pieces into the cornstarch, shake off the excess. Let rest for 5 to 10 minutes so the coating will stick to the meat. While the meat is resting, prep the remaining ingredients.

In a wok over high heat, heat the vegetable and sesame oils. Sauté the beef a few pieces at a time until just done, with the outsides beginning to crisp; transfer to a bowl and set aside. Once the meat has been removed, add the ginger and garlic. Sauté for approximately 1 minute; the oil remaining in the wok should become very fragrant. Add the soy sauce, water, Maggi seasoning, brown sugar, and vinegar. Stir until the sauce thickens, return the meat to the pan, and add the mushrooms. Stir-fry for another minute or so and then add half the chopped green onions. To serve, sprinkle the remaining green onions over the Mongolian beef.

YIELD: 2 SERVINGS

Chicken Tenders

The Saltgrass Steakhouse in known for delicious steaks, but did you know that they also make very good chicken tenders? These are dredged in seasoned flour and dipped in buttermilk to make them extra crispy.

vegetable oil, for frying

1 pound chicken tenders

1 cup all-purpose flour

1 teaspoon salt

½ teaspoon ground black pepper

½ cup buttermilk

½ cup water

Heat the oil to 350°F in a saucepan or add enough oil to cover the bottom 2 to 3 inches of a deep-fryer. Prepare seasoned flour by combining the flour, salt, and pepper in a shallow bowl. In another small bowl, combine the buttermilk and water. Dredge each chicken tender in the seasoned flour, then dip in the buttermilk mixture, and then dredge again in the flour, shaking off the excess. Carefully drop the coated chicken tenders into the oil and cook for 5 to 6 minutes, or until golden brown. Fry only a few at a time so they cook evenly and the temperature of the oil does not drop rapidly.

YIELD: 2 OR 3 SERVINGS

Orchard Chicken Salad

Even Subway has a seasonal menu. I think their Orchard Chicken Salad is one of their best items. Crunchy and crisp apples are surrounded by chicken, cherry-infused Craisins and much more. This recipe is made with light mayonnaise, so it helps save on calories.

1 red apple (Honeycrisp works well)

1 Granny Smith apple

1 tablespoon lemon juice

3 cups diced cooked chicken breast, in about ⅜-inch cubes

½ cup chopped celery

½ cup cherry juice–infused Craisins

1 to 1½ cups light mayonnaise

salt and pepper to taste

2 foot-long sub-style buns

toppings as desired, such as lettuce, pickles, onions, peppers

Core both the apples and chop into small cubes. Place in a bowl and sprinkle the lemon juice over apples; this will help keep them from turning brown. Add the chicken, celery, and Craisins, mixing well. Stir in 1 cup of mayonnaise; depending on how well the salad is coated, you may want to add an additional ½ cup. Season with salt and pepper. Refrigerate in a covered container for about an hour before serving to allow the flavors to marry. Assemble the sandwich by spreading mayonnaise on the sandwich bun, spooning in chicken salad, and topping with the fresh vegetables you desire.

YIELD: 2 FOOT-LONG SANDWICHES

TIP: After making this recipe a few times, I added some toasted almond slivers to this salad. They added a really nice crunch.

CopyKat.com's TACO BELL®

Bean Burritos

During my college years, this was a staple in my diet. Taco Bell was one of the few places where you could get pretty full on a couple of dollars. It's been a few years since I was in college, but these are still filling and inexpensive. A few years ago I lived in an area where there wasn't a Taco Bell, so I took matters into my own hands to make this bean burrito.

1 (8-ounce) can tomato sauce

⅓ cup water

¼ teaspoon chili powder

1½ teaspoons ground cumin

1½ teaspoons dried minced onions

1 tablespoon white vinegar

½ teaspoon garlic powder

½ teaspoon garlic salt

¼ teaspoon paprika

¼ teaspoon sugar

¼ teaspoon cayenne pepper

1 (16-ounce) can refried beans

3 (8-inch) round tortillas

¼ cup diced onion

½ cup shredded Cheddar cheese

In a small saucepan over medium-low heat, prepare the sauce by mixing together the first 11 ingredients (tomato sauce through cayenne pepper). Cook at a low simmer for 15 to 20 minutes. When you are ready to make the burritos, heat the refried beans in a small pan over low heat. One at a time, heat the tortillas in a warm skillet over low heat for about 30 seconds on each side. Top each tortilla with a third of the beans and a tablespoon or more of the sauce. Add the onions and shredded cheese, fold the tortilla sides over the filling, and roll up tightly.

YIELD: 3 BURRITOS

Five-Cheese Alfredo Sauce

Zio's is a wonderful place to go for freshly made Italian food. They have really good pizzas and pasta, and a five-cheese Alfredo sauce that's hard to beat. The cheeses combine to make the creamiest Alfredo sauce you can imagine.

1 pound dried pasta

4 cups heavy cream

½ cup salted butter

2¼ cups grated Parmesan cheese

¼ cup grated Asiago cheese

¼ cup shredded provolone cheese

½ cup shredded mozzarella cheese

freshly cracked pepper

Cook the pasta according to package directions. While it is cooking, in a large saucepan over medium-high heat, bring the cream and butter to a soft boil. Add the Parmesan cheese, and once it melts, turn the heat to low and add the remaining cheeses. Stir constantly until the cheeses melt. Add a few grinds of black pepper and serve immediately with the pasta.

YIELD: 6 TO 8 SERVINGS

Sides

Do you ever wish you could take home just the sides from your favorite restaurants? Sometimes I think the sides are the best part of the meal. Well, in this chapter you'll find many of your favorites. What I love about preparing restaurant side dishes at home is that finally you can get them in a larger quantity. At a restaurant, you might get an odd look if you ask for just a little bit more.

Included in this chapter are recipes that can help you at holiday time, such as a Boston Market sweet potato casserole that features a crispy, sweet, cookie-like crust. You can make green beans that taste like the ones you get at Texas Roadhouse, and if you've ever wanted to make Cheddar's Corn off the Cob, you can do that, too.

CopyKat.com's BENIHANA®

Fried Rice

At Benihana, you get a meal and a show. A skilled cook prepares your meal right in front of you in entertaining fashion, and the food is fantastic. One of the highlights is the expertly prepared fried rice.

½ cup (1 stick) butter, softened

1 tablespoon minced garlic

½ teaspoon dried parsley

2 teaspoons vegetable oil, divided

1 egg, beaten

¼ cup diced onions

1 tablespoon shredded carrot

1 tablespoon thinly sliced green onion

6 cups cooked long-grain white rice

½ teaspoon salt

½ teaspoon ground black pepper

2 teaspoons soy sauce

1 teaspoon sesame seeds

Ahead of time, prepare the garlic butter that will be used to season the rice. To the room-temperature butter, add the garlic and parsley, blending well.

Heat a grill to 350°F and drizzle 1 teaspoon oil onto the grill surface. Pour the beaten egg onto the grill and cook by continually chopping the egg until it is almost done. Add the remaining 1 teaspoon oil and sauté the onions, carrot, and green onion with the egg. After the onion begins to become translucent, add the cooked rice. Season with the salt, pepper, and soy sauce, and add a couple of tablespoons of the garlic butter. Stir and cook until the rice has browned and the onions have cooked through. Sprinkle the sesame seeds over the rice and serve.

Store the leftover garlic butter in an airtight container in the refrigerator for up to 4 days. You can reheat the fried rice in the microwave, but it is even better if you warm it in a skillet over medium heat with a touch of oil.

YIELD: 6 TO 8 SERVINGS

CopyKat.com's **BOSTON MARKET®**

Squash Casserole

My family has found that this casserole makes a great replacement for stuffing or potatoes in a meal.

1 (8½-ounce) box Jiffy corn muffin mix, prepared according to the directions on the box

4½ cups diced zucchini

4½ cups diced yellow squash

¾ cup (1½ sticks) butter

1½ cups chopped yellow onion

1 teaspoon salt

½ teaspoon ground black pepper

½ teaspoon dried thyme

1 tablespoon chopped fresh parsley

8 ounces American cheese, diced (use a store brand, not Velveeta)

3 cubes chicken bouillon

1 teaspoon minced garlic

Prepare the corn muffin mix as directed on the package, and set aside to cool. Place the zucchini and yellow squash in a large saucepan with just enough water to cover. Cook over medium-low heat just until tender, 7 to 8 minutes. Remove from the heat and drain, reserving 1 cup of the cooking liquid.

Preheat the oven to 350°F. Spray an 11 x 13-inch baking pan with nonstick spray.

In a large saucepan over medium-low heat, melt the butter. Sauté the onions in the butter until they turn translucent and then add the salt, pepper, thyme, and parsley. Add the bouillon cubes and garlic, stirring to dissolve the bouillon. Stir in the drained squash and diced cheese. Crumble the cornbread into the mixture, pour in the reserved 1 cup cooking liquid, and mix well.

Cover with foil and bake for 50 to 60 minutes. Remove the cover for the last 20 minutes, until the top starts to brown and is hot and bubbling.

YIELD: 8 TO 10 SERVINGS

Sweet Potato Casserole

Sweet potato casserole is many people's favorite holiday side dish. What makes the Boston Market version extra special is the cookie-like topping, and it doesn't stop there; under the cookie crust, a layer of marshmallows adds sweet, melting goodness. You can prepare this using either fresh sweet potatoes or canned sweet potato purée. Serving a lot of people? This is the perfect recipe for you.

4½ to 5 pounds sweet potatoes, or 5 pounds canned sweet potato purée

¾ cup (1½ sticks) butter, softened, divided

2 large eggs

1¼ teaspoons salt, divided

1½ teaspoons ground cinnamon, divided

½ teaspoon grated nutmeg

½ teaspoon vanilla extract

1½ cups packed dark brown sugar, divided

¼ cup heavy cream

2 cups miniature marshmallows

½ cup all-purpose flour

1 cup quick-cooking rolled oats

Preheat the oven to 350°F and spray a 9 x 13-inch baking pan with cooking spray. If you are using raw sweet potatoes, line a rimmed baking sheet with foil and wrap the potatoes individually in foil. Place on the lined baking sheet and bake for about 1 hour. Test with a fork; if you can pierce the potatoes easily, they are done. Let cool until you can handle them, and then remove the foil and push off the skins. Place the cooked potatoes in a large bowl.

Using a blender or hand masher, mash the baked sweet potatoes (or the canned sweet potato purée) with ¼ cup butter until they are mostly smooth. Add the eggs, 1 teaspoon salt, 1 teaspoon cinnamon, nutmeg, and vanilla and blend until you have a uniform mixture. Mix in ½ cup brown sugar and the cream.

To make the "oatmeal cookie" streusel topping, in a medium bowl stir together the flour, 1 cup brown sugar, oats, ½ teaspoon cinnamon, and

¼ teaspoon salt. Using a fork, cut in the ½ cup softened butter until you have a crumbly mixture.

Assemble the casserole by spreading the sweet potato mixture into the prepared pan. Top with the marshmallows, and then sprinkle the oatmeal topping over the marshmallows. Bake at 350°F for 30 to 45 minutes, or until the marshmallows are completely melted.

YIELD: 10 TO 12 SERVINGS

Hush Puppies

Captain D's serves fine restaurant–quality seafood. I also think they have some of the best sides around. Their hushpuppies are hard to beat—tender on the inside, filled with tiny bits of diced onion. My tip here is to use oil in which you've previously fried fish. That way the hushpuppies will pick up a little extra flavor.

4 to 6 cups vegetable oil for frying	2 teaspoons sugar
2 cups self-rising white cornmeal mix	1½ tablespoons diced white or yellow onion
1 cup yellow cornmeal	½ teaspoon salt
1½ cups buttermilk	

Pour the oil into a deep fryer or saucepan to a depth of 3 to 4 inches, and heat the oil to 350°F. In a medium bowl, stir together the white cornmeal mix, yellow cornmeal, buttermilk, sugar, diced onion, and salt. Drop by a 1-ounce (2-tablespoon) cookie scoop into the hot oil. Fry for 1 to 2 minutes, rotating the hushpuppies as necessary so they fry golden brown on all sides. Fry only a few at a time for the best results. If you add too many in at once the temperature of the oil will drop and the results will be poor. Drain on paper towels and serve hot.

YIELD: 10 TO 12 SERVINGS

CopyKat.com's **CHEDDAR'S CASUAL CAFE®**

Sweet Corn off the Cob

One of the things I love most about Cheddar's is they serve up home-style meals, and they make some of the best side dishes around, like this buttery sweet corn. Best of all, it's made from frozen corn, so you can have that fresh corn-off-the-cob taste any time of year.

1 (16-ounce) package frozen corn	2 teaspoons sugar
½ cup plus 1 tablespoon water, divided	½ teaspoon salt
3 tablespoons butter	1 teaspoon cornstarch

In a small saucepan over medium heat, combine the frozen corn, ½ cup water, and butter. Heat until the corn is heated through. Stir in the sugar and salt. In a small bowl, mix the cornstarch in 1 tablespoon water until smooth. Add to the corn in the saucepan and bring to a boil, stirring occasionally until heated through.

YIELD: 4 SERVINGS

Baked Potato Casserole

Dickey's Barbecue has been around since the 1940s. They spend hours smoking their meat, and if you've never tried their barbecue, you're missing out on wonderful smoked goodness. In addition, they serve many delicious side dishes. This baked potato casserole brings all of the flavor of a loaded baked potato in an easy-to-prepare casserole. While the restaurant serves this in individual proportions, you can make it in a casserole dish for your family.

4 large russet potatoes

¼ cup (½ stick) butter

½ cup sour cream

¼ cup milk

1 teaspoon salt

½ teaspoon ground black pepper

⅓ cup "real bacon bits," cooked and crumbled, divided

½ cup shredded Cheddar cheese

¼ cup sliced green onion tops

Preheat the oven to 425°F. Scrub the potatoes clean and bake for 1 hour. It is not necessary to poke holes in the potatoes; in fact, if you don't, they will be light and fluffy on the inside. When they have cooled enough to handle, scoop out the white flesh and place in a bowl. Using an electric mixer, mash until smooth, then beat in the butter, sour cream, and milk. Mix in the salt and pepper and about 1 tablespoon of the bacon bits. Spoon the potatoes into a 2-quart casserole dish that has been sprayed with cooking spray. Garnish with the remaining bacon bits, shredded cheese, and green onion tops.

YIELD: 8 SERVINGS

CopyKat.com's **DICKEY'S BARBECUE PIT™**

Jalapeño Beans

This recipe can help spice up ordinary canned beans into something a little more flavorful.

2 (15-ounce) cans ranch-style beans

½ jalapeño pepper, finely diced

½ teaspoon ground black pepper

In a medium saucepan over medium-low heat, stir together the beans, jalapeño, and black pepper.

YIELD: 6 SERVINGS

TIP: You can adjust the spiciness to your own taste. If you like more heat, you can add more jalapeño pepper, or leave the seeds in when you cut it, or add more jalapeño; if you like less heat, use a little less jalapeño.

CopyKat.com's **DOUBLE DAVE'S PIZZAWORKS®**

Pepperoni Pizza Rolls

Double Dave's is known for so many special dishes. I think their pizza rolls are some of the best around, made with two different types of cheese and pepperoni. These aren't hard to make, and in a few minutes you can have delicious pizza rolls.

1 pound pizza dough

4 to 6 slices provolone cheese

15 pepperoni slices

ranch dressing or pizza sauce, for serving

Preheat the oven to 450°F. Roll out the pizza dough very thin to make a large round approximately ¼ inch thick. Arrange slices of cheese and then slices of pepperoni on the dough. Cut as you'd cut a pizza, into 8 slices. Roll each slice from the outside edge toward the center or small end. Press the edges together to seal. Place on an ungreased baking sheet and bake for 10 to 15 minutes, or until golden brown. Serve with your favorite ranch dressing or pizza sauce.

YIELD: 4 SERVINGS

Carrot Soufflé

If you've never had a carrot soufflé, you are missing out. This light and fluffy side dish will turn those who profess to dislike carrots into fans who want you to prepare this recipe over and over again.

6 cups carrot pieces (about 2 pounds, peeled and cut in 1-inch pieces)

½ cup butter, melted

1¼ cups sugar

1½ teaspoons baking powder

1 teaspoon vanilla extract

½ teaspoon salt

4 eggs, beaten

powdered sugar

Preheat the oven to 350°F and spray a 2-quart casserole dish with cooking spray. Place the carrots in a medium pot, cover with water, and cook over medium-high heat for about 15 minutes, or until a fork easily pierces a carrot. Drain and transfer to a mixing bowl. Use an electric mixer or a potato masher to purée the carrots. Once they are smooth, blend in the melted butter, sugar, baking powder, vanilla, and salt. Combine the beaten eggs with the carrot mixture and pour into a 2-quart casserole dish. Bake for 30 minutes. Remove from the oven, let cool for 5 to 10 minutes, and dust with powdered sugar to serve.

YIELD: 8 SERVINGS

CopyKat.com's LOGAN'S ROADHOUSE®

Fried Shrooms

If you have never been to Logan's Roadhouse, you'll know that it's a fun restaurant that serves delicious steaks and some of the best rolls around, and they have roasted and salted peanuts to munch on while your food is being prepared. These mushrooms are battered and fried until browned and crispy—when you make them, there won't be any left over.

6 cups vegetable oil, for frying

2 cups all-purpose flour

2 teaspoons salt

1 tablespoon ground black pepper

2 cups buttermilk

1 pound white mushrooms, stems removed

Pour the oil into a deep fryer or saucepan to a depth of 3 to 4 inches, and heat the oil to 350°F. In a medium bowl, stir together the flour, salt, and pepper so that the seasonings are evenly distributed. Pour the buttermilk into a small bowl. Dredge the mushrooms in the seasoned flour, dip into the buttermilk, and dredge in the flour again. Shake off the excess flour and place the breaded mushroom on a plate. Allow the mushrooms to rest for a couple of minutes before frying. Fry the mushrooms for 2 to 3 minutes, or until golden brown on all sides. Drain on a wire rack before serving.

YIELD: 4 SERVINGS

Skillet Cabbage

Luby's skillet cabbage is cooked with bacon and seasoned just right with salt and pepper—this is almost foolproof to make.

- 1 large head green cabbage
- 3 cups water
- 6 ounces bacon, cut into 1-inch pieces

- 1 teaspoon ground black pepper
- 1 teaspoon salt
- 3 tablespoons butter

Remove the cabbage core and discard. Slice the cabbage into 1 to 2-inch pieces; you should have approximately 12 cups. Place in a large pot along with the bacon and water. Bring the water to a boil over medium-high heat and then reduce the heat to a medium-low. Add the pepper and salt to the pot, cover with a lid, and simmer for about 30 minutes, stirring occasionally. Before serving, stir in the butter.

YIELD: 8 SERVINGS

Baked Tots

Sure, anyone can cover Tater Tots with cheese, but leave it to James Coney Island to take this one step further. They smother theirs with cheese and bacon, heat them in the oven until the cheese melts, and then top them with sour cream and green onions. Tater Tots have never looked or tasted so good.

4 cups vegetable oil, for frying

8 ounces frozen Tater Tots

½ cup shredded Cheddar cheese

2 tablespoons crumbled cooked bacon

1 tablespoon sour cream

2 teaspoons sliced green onion

Preheat the oven to 350°F and spray a small casserole dish with cooking spray. Pour the oil into a deep fryer or saucepan to a depth of 3 to 4 inches, and heat the oil to 350°F. Cook half of the Tater Tots in the hot oil until golden brown; this should take 2 to 4 minutes. Once the first batch is finished, drain on paper towels and then cook the remaining tots. Place in a the prepared casserole dish and sprinkle the cheese and bacon over them. Heat in the oven for 5 to 7 minutes, or until the cheese begins to melt. Remove from the oven and top with the sour cream and green onions.

∞∞∞∞∞∞∞∞∞∞∞∞∞∞∞∞∞∞∞∞∞∞
YIELD: 2 SERVINGS

French Fries with Cheese

We all have guilty pleasures in life. These cheese fries are one of mine. Many restaurants offer unique cheese fries with delicious cheeses, but these are fun, prepared with cheese from a pressurized can or "fromage jet" as some call it. Before you say "no way," give it a try. I think these are great with ketchup.

4 to 6 cups vegetable oil, for frying	salt
frozen French fries	cheese in a can

Pour the oil into a deep fryer or sauce pan to a depth of 2 to 4 inches and heat the oil to 350°F. Fry the French fries until golden brown, then transfer them to a wire rack to dry. (If you use a rack instead of paper towels, the fries will have a crisper texture.) Salt the fries while they are still warm. Place a serving of fries on a plate and top with cheese from a can.

YIELD: VARIES

CopyKat.com's KFC®

Coleslaw

This classic coleslaw from KFC is so easy to make, and it stays fresh for days. In fact, this is one of those dishes that actually tastes better the second or even the third day.

10 cups diced green cabbage

1 cup diced green bell pepper

½ cup grated white onion

½ cup shredded carrot

2 cups Miracle Whip Light dressing

½ cup sugar

¼ cup white vinegar

¼ cup vegetable oil

In a large bowl, mix together the diced cabbage, bell pepper, onion, and carrot. In a separate small bowl, prepare the coleslaw dressing by mixing together the Miracle Whip Light, sugar, vinegar, and oil. Pour the dressing over the cabbage mixture and stir to combine well. Let the salad rest in an airtight container in the refrigerator. This will stay fresh for up to a week.

YIELD: 10 TO 12 SERVINGS

Roasted Butternut Squash

I was pleasantly surprised at the Olive Garden to find a side dish that didn't involve pasta. My waiter told me that this was one of the most popular sides currently on the menu. Roasted butternut squash is easy to prepare, and you can even buy the squash already cut up. This squash is made extra special because it is cooked in a sweet white wine.

1 butternut squash, cubed (about 6 to 8 cups)

2 tablespoons vegetable oil

1 teaspoon salt

1 cup sweet white wine (Riesling works well)

Preheat the oven to 400°F and spray a 9 x 13-inch baking dish with cooking spray. In a bowl, toss the butternut squash with the oil and salt. Spread on a rimmed baking sheet and bake for 30 minutes. Transfer the squash pieces to the prepared baking dish. Pour in the wine. Bake until the squash is tender, 15 to 20 more minutes—the smaller the squash pieces, the shorter the cooking time.

YIELD: 4 TO 6 SERVINGS

CopyKat.com's **OUTBACK STEAKHOUSE®**

Baked Potato

Sure, we all know how to bake a baked potato. But do you know how to get the crisp skin and wonderful salted crust that the ones at Outback Steakhouse have? These are made just a little differently than your everyday baked potato. These potatoes are rubbed with vegetable oil before baking. There's no need to pierce the potato—we want to keep all the moisture on the inside so the potato will be nice and fluffy. Once you try making baked potatoes like this, I bet you won't go back to the old way.

4 (8-ounce) russet potatoes

½ cup vegetable oil

1 to 2 tablespoons kosher salt

Preheat the oven to 450°F. Wash and dry the potatoes. Pour the vegetable oil into a small dish, dip a paper towel into the oil, and rub oil over each potato. Place the potatoes on a baking sheet and sprinkle kosher salt over them. Bake for approximately 1 hour. Check for doneness by inserting a fork; if it pierces the potato easily, the potato is done.

YIELD: 4 SERVINGS

CopyKat.com's **OUTBACK STEAKHOUSE®**

Sweet Potato with Honey Butter

I can't stop with just one baked potato. I need to show you how to make Outback's baked sweet potato as well. I like this one better than similar potatoes at other steakhouses. Why? They use real butter in their honey butter, which makes all of the difference. You'll have enough honey butter for lots of sweet potatoes, or you can use it on toast, rolls, or even homemade French toast.

1 small sweet potato (about 6 ounces)

2 cups (4 sticks) butter, softened

¼ cup honey

1 tablespoon dark brown sugar

½ teaspoon ground cinnamon

Preheat the oven to 375°F. Wash the sweet potato and wrap it with foil. Place on a baking sheet and bake for approximately 1 hour, or until you can easily pierce the potato with a fork. While the potato is baking, use a blender to mix together the butter and honey until the texture is uniform. To serve, remove the foil and split the potato open with a knife. Top with the brown sugar, cinnamon, and finally a scoop of the honey butter. Store leftover honey butter in the refrigerator, covered.

YIELD: 1 SERVING, PLUS EXTRA HONEY BUTTER

CopyKat.com's OUTBACK STEAKHOUSE®

Steamed Green Beans

Many followers of the CopyKat website requested this recipe. You may be asking yourself, how can you make green beans extra special? The Outback Steakhouse steams them, which really helps preserve the fresh flavor. They are then seasoned with a sweet, garlic, and buttery sauce that will turn those people who dislike green vegetables into those who ask for seconds.

1 pound fresh green beans (French green beans, or haricots verts, are best)

¼ cup (½ stick) butter

2 tablespoons dark brown sugar

½ teaspoon Maggi seasoning (or you can substitute soy sauce)

½ teaspoon garlic powder

¼ teaspoon salt

¼ teaspoon freshly ground black pepper

Trim the steam ends off of the green beans. Steam the green beans in either a steamer or your microwave until they are just done; you want them still firm. In my microwave, it takes about 2 minutes to steam them.

While the green beans are steaming, begin making the seasoned butter sauce. In a small saucepan over medium-low heat, combine the butter, brown sugar, Maggi seasoning, garlic powder, salt, and pepper. Stir until the butter is melted and the brown sugar is completely dissolved.

Drain the steamed green beans and place in a bowl. Add the butter mixture and stir until the beans are coated with the butter seasoning.

YIELD: 4 SERVINGS

CopyKat.com's **PANERA BREAD®**

Macaroni and Cheese

There's nothing more comforting than a big plate of macaroni and cheese. White Cheddar cheese gives Panera Bread's creamy version of mac and cheese a distinctive flavor that's hard not to love.

- 1 (16-ounce) box small shell pasta
- 3 tablespoons butter
- 3 tablespoons all-purpose flour
- 2½ cups half-and-half
- 3 ounces white American cheese (this can be purchased at the deli counter; not Velveeta)
- 6 ounces aged white Cheddar cheese
- 2 teaspoons Dijon mustard
- ½ teaspoon dry mustard
- ½ teaspoon salt
- ¼ teaspoon Tabasco sauce

Prepare the pasta according to the package directions; drain and set aside. While the pasta is cooking, make the cheese sauce. In a medium saucepan over medium heat, melt the butter. Add the flour; stir and cook for 2 to 3 minutes. The flour mixture should begin to smell like piecrust. Raise the heat to medium-high and slowly add the half-and-half, stirring vigorously as you do; the half-and-half should thicken. Reduce the heat to medium-low and add the cheeses, stirring until they melt completely. Stir in the Dijon and dry mustard, salt, and Tabasco. Transfer the drained macaroni to a bowl and pour the cheese sauce over it. Serve immediately.

YIELD: 4 SERVINGS

CopyKat.com's **PICCADILLY CAFETERIA™**

Broccoli Rice Casserole

Often broccoli rice casserole is made with American cheese, and sometimes it's overpowered by an abundance of the cheese. The Piccadilly Cafeteria only adds the cheese on top, and they use a quality Cheddar.

2 (10.5-ounce) cans condensed cream of mushroom soup	6 cups cooked long-grain rice
2 soup cans of milk	3 cups chopped steamed broccoli
	3 cups shredded Cheddar cheese

Preheat the oven to 350°F. Prepare the mushroom soup on the stovetop, using the milk and following the directions on the can. In a large bowl, combine the soup with the cooked rice and steamed broccoli. Stir to blend well. Pour the mixture into a 9 x 13-inch baking dish. Sprinkle the cheese over the top and bake for about 35 minutes.

YIELD: 8 SERVINGS

TIP: You can buy American cheese at most deli counters. You can purchase it already sliced, but any grocery store with a deli department can sell you this cheese. It melts wonderfully and will not break apart like Cheddar cheese can.

Cream Gravy

Piccadilly Cafeteria is a well-known chain in the South. I love their basic cooking from scratch. Everything tastes like your grandmother made it. This recipe similar to their basic cream-style gravy. You can use this on biscuits, chicken-fried steak, mashed potatoes, and so much more.

2 tablespoon butter

2 tablespoons flour

1¾ cups whole milk

½ teaspoon salt

¼ ground black pepper

In a medium saucepan over medium heat, combine the butter and flour. Cook the butter and flour together until they form a nice paste, stirring constantly. When the paste develops a nutty, fragrant smell, 2 to 3 minutes, slowly add the whole milk. The mixture will begin to thicken. Once all of the milk is added, turn the heat down to a simmer, and season with the salt and pepper. Allow the gravy to reduce by one-third, about 15 minutes.

YIELD: 1¼ CUPS

CopyKat.com's SWEET TOMATOES®

Lemon Greek Penne Pasta

This would be a perfect recipe to make for a Meatless Monday. The sauce is rich and creamy, like an Alfredo sauce, but the lemon really adds a nice touch. It would also go very well with a piece of grilled fish. This dish tastes best freshly made, but if you're going save any leftovers, store the pasta and the sauce separately, and bring them together when you're ready to enjoy the meal again.

12 ounces dried penne pasta

½ cup (1 stick) butter

2 cups heavy cream

1 cup grated Parmesan cheese, plus more for garnish if desired

1½ tablespoons freshly squeezed lemon juice

½ teaspoon grated lemon zest

½ teaspoon ground black pepper

salt to taste

minced parsley or capers, for garnish (optional)

Cook the pasta according to the package directions. Meanwhile, in a medium saucepan over medium-high heat, melt the butter and then whisk in the cream. When the mixture begins to bubble, stir in the Parmesan cheese; continue stirring until the sauce is well blended and the cheese has melted. Stir in the lemon juice and zest and season with pepper and salt.

Drain the cooked pasta and transfer it to a bowl. Pour the sauce over the pasta and toss to mix well. If you wish, garnish with additional Parmesan, parsley, or even a few capers.

YIELD: 4 SERVINGS

CopyKat.com's **TEXAS ROADHOUSE™**

Rolls

Honestly, I don't think you can find a better roll out there than the hot fresh rolls from the Texas Roadhouse. Now you can prepare these wonderfully sweet and light rolls to serve with your favorite meal.

1 cup warm milk (100°F)

1 package or 2¼ teaspoons active dry yeast

⅓ cup sugar

3½ cups all-purpose flour, plus more for board

1 egg

⅓ cup butter, melted plus ¼ cup (½ stick) butter, melted (optional)

1 teaspoon salt

In a cup or small bowl, stir together the warm milk, sugar, and yeast. Allow the yeast to proof and begin to activate while you prepare the other ingredients. Using a stand mixer or food processor, combine the flour, egg, ⅓ cup melted butter, and salt. Add the milk mixture and process until you have a smooth dough; it will be stickier and wetter than regular bread dough. Place the dough in a greased bowl, turn the dough to grease all sides, and cover with a towel. Let rise until it has doubled in size.

When the dough has doubled, punch it down and turn it out on a floured board. Let rest for 10 minutes. Roll out the dough into a large, flat rectangle approximately ½ inch thick. Cut into about 16 portions with a sharp knife and place on a greased baking sheet and let rise again, until doubled. Preheat the oven to 375°F. Bake the rolls for 10 minutes on the greased baking sheet. They will be light brown when removed from the oven. If desired you can brush the tops of the rolls with the remaining ¼ cup melted butter before serving.

YIELD: ABOUT 16 ROLLS

Green Beans

Texas Roadhouse Grill makes the green beans you wished your grandmother would have made. The real secret here is to add bacon while you cook the beans, and then add a little more when you serve them up. Be sure to buy thick, lean bacon for this recipe; it's the thick bacon that really does the trick.

8 thick bacon slices

1 (1-pound) package frozen green beans

2 cups water

¼ cup diced white onion

1 teaspoon sugar

1 teaspoon chicken base

¼ cup (½ stick) butter

¾ teaspoon ground black pepper

salt to taste

Fry all the bacon, but remove 4 of the pieces when they are done but not yet crisp; allow the remaining strips to crisp fully. Chop the 4 not-crisp pieces and place in a medium saucepan with the green beans, water, and diced onion. Add the sugar, chicken base, butter, and black pepper. Simmer over low heat for 10 to 15 minutes, or until the beans are cooked. Just before serving, crumble the crisped bacon and add it to the beans. Taste the green beans and adjust seasoning with salt and pepper. I find that often the bacon salts this dish enough. It is not necessary to drain the liquid when serving the beans.

YIELD: 4 SERVINGS.

TIP: Chicken base is an ingredient like bouillon cubes, but it offers more flavor and less salt. It is sold in most grocery stores right next to the bouillon cubes.

Jasmine Rice

If you've never picked up a bag of jasmine rice, you're in for a pleasant surprise. This is a wonderfully fragrant long-grain rice that isn't as sticky as some kinds, with grains that stay nicely separated. Add a few simple ingredients, and you have a wonderful side dish.

2 cups jasmine rice

2½ cups water

½ cup coconut milk

1 cup diced red bell pepper

½ cup diced yellow onion

2 tablespoons butter

3 tablespoons chopped fresh parsley

1 teaspoon salt

Steam the rice in a rice cooker with the water and coconut milk, following the steamer manufacturer's directions. The rice could also be cooked on the stovetop in a saucepan by bringing the water and coconut milk to boil in a saucepan and then adding the rice. Cover with a lid, reduce the heat to a simmer, and cook for 18 to 25 minutes. While the rice cooks, sauté the bell pepper and onion with the butter in a saucepan over medium heat; continue cooking until the onions are translucent. In a serving bowl, combine the cooked rice with the sautéed onions and bell peppers. Stir in the chopped parsley and salt and serve immediately.

YIELD: 6 SERVINGS

Dessert

I think one of the things that makes dining out special is dessert. Growing up, dessert was a rare treat. I don't know why, but there's always something magical about dessert, whether it involves ice cream, chocolate, or something else.

You'll find a wide variety of desserts in this chapter. I'll show you how to wow your guests with a cake that oozes a fountain of chocolate. How about a pumpkin cheesecake, or turnovers to impress your friends and family? Armed with this chapter, you can serve complex or simple desserts that everyone can enjoy.

CopyKat.com's

1-2-3 Jell-O®

Perhaps you are a product of the 1980s, like me, when Jell-O came out with so many creative desserts. One of my favorites was the 1-2-3 Jell-O that actually separated into three different layers. I love to serve this in wineglasses to make it look extra fancy. You definitely want to use clear serving dishes, so you can see the different layers.

1 (4-serving) package gelatin dessert mix (any flavor)

¾ cup boiling water

ice cubes

½ cup cold water

½ cup thawed frozen whipped topping (Cool Whip or similar)

In a heatproof bowl, dissolve the gelatin mix in the boiling water. Add enough ice cubes to the cold water to measure 1¼ cups; add to the gelatin mixture. Pour into a blender container, cover, and blend for 30 seconds. Add the whipped topping and blend until smooth.

Divide evenly among 4 dessert dishes. Refrigerate for at least 20 minutes, or until set.

YIELD: 4 SERVINGS

CopyKat.com's APPLEBEE'S®

Triple Chocolate Meltdown®

I love chocolate lava cake with its gooey center, and Applebee's version is *so* good. White chocolate is drizzled over the lava cake, and semisweet chocolate is drizzled over ice cream on top of the cake.

⅔ cup semisweet chocolate chips (4 ounces)

½ cup (1 stick) butter, plus more for the ramekins

2 large eggs

2 large egg yolks

¼ cup sugar, plus more for dusting the ramekins

2 tablespoons all-purpose flour

¼ teaspoon salt

4 ounces white chocolate

4 ounces semisweet chocolate

2 teaspoons vegetable shortening, divided

4 large scoops vanilla ice cream

Preheat the oven to 450°F. Butter 4 small (6-ounce) ramekins or other small ovenproof dishes, then dust with sugar. In the top of a double boiler over simmering water, melt the ⅔ cup chocolate chips with the ½ cup butter, whisking occasionally, until smooth and uniform. Meanwhile, whisk together the whole eggs, yolks, and ¼ cup sugar until light and fluffy.

Pour the melted chocolate mixture into the egg mixture and stir very quickly. Add the flour and salt and blend until just mixed. Pour into the prepared ramekins. Set the ramekins on a baking sheet and bake for 8 minutes; the cake centers will still be soft. Invert each chocolate lava cake onto a dessert plate. They will slip out of the ramekins in a few seconds.

To make the drizzle toppings, place the white and semisweet chocolates in separate bowls and add 1 teaspoon shortening to each bowl. Melt in the microwave on low in 15-second increments: microwave the chocolate, stir, and microwave again until fully melted.

To assemble the desserts, top each lava cake with a scoop of ice cream. Drizzle the white chocolate over the cake and drizzle the semisweet chocolate on the ice cream.

YIELD: 4 SERVINGS

CopyKat.com's ARBY'S®

Cherry Turnover

Arby's serves some of the best turnovers around. Using store-bought puff pastry, you can make turnovers just like theirs. Most grocery stores sell puff pastry, and some specialty stores sell it cut into smaller squares. If you can only find the sheets, you'll need to cut them to size yourself.

12 (4 x 4-inch) puff pastry squares

1 (21-ounce) can cherry pie filling

1 egg white lightly beaten with 1 teaspoon water, for egg wash

3 to 4 tablespoons milk

1 cup powdered sugar

Preheat the oven to 375°F. Lay out the puff pastry squares on an ungreased baking sheets. Place about 2 tablespoons cherry pie filling in the center of each square; ideally, there will be 5 or 6 cherries in each turnover. Fold over the turnover to make a triangle. "Glue" the triangle together by brushing the egg wash on all the inside edges of the pastry except for about 1 inch at the middle point to leave a vent. Gently press the edges together—don't mash them. Brush the top side of each turnover with the egg wash. Bake for 25 to 27 minutes, or until lightly browned. Remove from the oven and allow to cool slightly.

Make the frosting by combining the milk and the powdered sugar in a bowl to make a thin frosting. Drizzle frosting over the turnovers.

YIELD: 12 TURNOVERS

CopyKat.com's ARBY'S®

Chocolate Turnover

The first time I had this chocolate dessert, I was amazed. This is just a bargain when it comes to a tasty dessert: a rich chocolate ganache surrounded by a flaky crust. Honestly, I've had desserts like this at very fancy restaurants.

10 ounces semisweet chocolate (60% cacao is my personal favorite)

3 tablespoons butter

8 (4 x 4-inch) puff pastry squares

1 egg white lightly beaten with 1 teaspoon water, for egg wash

Preheat the oven to 375°F. In a small saucepan over medium-low heat, gently heat together the chocolate and butter. Do not allow the chocolate to scorch. Stir frequently, and when the chocolate has melted all the way through, remove it from the stovetop and set it aside.

Lay out the puff pastry squares on an ungreased baking sheet. Spoon about 1½ tablespoons of melted chocolate mixture in the center of each square. (You will have some left over; this will make the chocolate drizzle for the turnover tops.) Fold over the turnover to make a triangle. "Glue" the triangle together by brushing the egg wash on all the inside edges of the pastry except for about 1 inch at the middle point to leave a vent. Gently press the edges together—don't mash them. Brush the top side of each turnover with the egg wash. Bake for 25 to 27 minutes, or until lightly browned. Transfer from the baking sheet to a wire rack and let cool slightly. While still warm, drizzle the remaining chocolate over the tops of the turnovers.

YIELD: 8 TURNOVERS

CopyKat.com's BIG BOY®

Strawberry Pie

One way you can enjoy fresh strawberries in the spring is in a strawberry pie. This one is easy to make, and you can always use refrigerated pie dough if you don't want to make yours from scratch. Serve the pie with whipped cream.

CRUST

1 cup all-purpose flour

½ cup (1 stick) butter

3 tablespoon powdered sugar

1 teaspoon vanilla extract

ice-cold water

FILLING

2 tablespoons cornstarch

1 cup water

¾ cup granulated sugar

¼ teaspoon salt

¼ teaspoon red food coloring

1 pound strawberries, stemmed and quartered (about 3 cups)

TO MAKE THE CRUST: Preheat the oven to 350°F. Make the crust by cutting the butter together with the flour and powdered sugar. When the dough forms pieces the size of small peas, work in the vanilla and a teaspoon or two of cold water until the dough can be pressed into a 9-inch pie pan. Prick the pie dough all over with a fork and bake for 10 to 12 minutes, or until the crust has become a light golden color. Set aside to cool.

TO MAKE THE FILLING: Blend the cornstarch into the water. Place in a medium saucepan with the sugar and salt and cook over medium heat for about 5 minutes, stirring constantly, until thickened. Stir in the food coloring and remove from the stovetop.

When the crust is cool, fill it with the berries, piling them higher in the center. Pour the thickened filling mixture over the berries and place the pie in the refrigerator. Allow the pie to set up for at least 1 hour before serving.

YIELD: 8 SERVINGS

Reese's® Peanut Butter Pie

I love Baskin-Robbins. Growing up, I used to ride my bicycle a couple of miles just to get to one of these ice cream parlors. I love their chocolate and peanut butter flavor, but the peanut butter–cup pie is definitely one of my favorites. This pie would cost you almost thirty dollars in the store, but you can make it at home it for far less.

1 quart Baskin-Robbins Peanut Butter 'n Chocolate (or your favorite flavor)

1 cup prepared hot fudge topping

1 prepared 9-inch chocolate cookie crumb pie crust

2 full-size Reese's Peanut Butter Cups

1 cup whipped cream

Allow the ice cream to sit out long enough to soften, but don't let it melt! Warm the hot fudge topping slightly in a saucepan over low heat for ease of spreading and spread about half of it into the bottom of the crumb crust. Mash the ice cream carefully over the hot fudge topping, spreading it evenly over the pie. Place the pie in the freezer for a few hours. Also place the peanut butter cups in the freezer.

Remove the pie from the freezer. Warm the remaining hot fudge topping, but not so much that it will melt the ice cream. Spread the topping over the ice cream. To serve, space 8 dollops of frosting or whipped cream around the pie. Place the pie back into freezer and let the pie set for about 25 minutes before serving. Cut the frozen peanut butter cups into quarters and place a quarter in each dollop. Slice into 8 pieces.

YIELD: 8 SERVINGS

TIP: You can use your favorite frosting on this ice cream pie in place of the whipped cream. Chocolate frosting goes very well.

CopyKat.com's

Ice Cream Bonbons

Who hasn't entered the fantasy of being able to lie around all day eating ice cream bonbons? These take some effort to make, but they are very good. At the grocery store, you can only buy bonbons in a couple of flavors, but you can make them at home with any flavor of ice cream you want. It is important to note that you will need to work in multiple steps; keeping the ice cream frozen solid is the key.

1 quart ice cream	2 tablespoons vegetable shortening
12 ounces semisweet chocolate chips	sprinkles, finely chopped nuts, or other toppings (optional)

Start by placing a baking sheet in the freezer for about 30 minutes before using. Once it's chilled, you can begin to scoop the ice cream. Use a small cookie scoop to form ice cream balls. Work very quickly, and move the scooped balls into the freezer if they begin to melt. Leave the ice cream balls in the freezer for 6 to 8 hours. They must be frozen solid before you coat them with warm chocolate on top, or the chocolate will slide right off.

Gently heat the chocolate chips and shortening together in the top of a double boiler, stirring until smooth. Remove from the heat and allow to cool for 5 to 7 minutes. If the chocolate is too hot, it will melt the ice cream immediately.

Working very quickly, pick up an ice cream ball by resting it on a fork. Hold it over the melted chocolate and spoon chocolate over the ice cream, letting the excess drip off. Quickly set the ball down on the baking sheet and work on the next ice cream ball. Time is of the essence—work quickly. If you want to sprinkle on nuts, sprinkles, or other toppings, do so while the chocolate is still "wet" and not fully set. Pop the bonbons back into the freezer for about 2 hours before serving.

YIELD: 6 TO 8 SERVINGS

CopyKat.com's **COCO'S BAKERY RESTAURANT®**

Nutella™ Crêpes

Crêpes are wonderfully diverse. You can make them sweet or savory, and the filling possibilities are endless.

2 cups all-purpose flour

2 large eggs

2 tablespoons vegetable oil, divided

1 teaspoon salt

2 cups milk

1 teaspoon vanilla extract

½ cup Nutella

powdered sugar, for dusting

Put the flour in a bowl and make a well in the center. Add the eggs to the well in the flour along with 1 tablespoon of the vegetable oil, the salt, and ½ cup of the milk; blend into the flour until smooth. Mix in the rest of the milk and the vanilla. Let the batter rest in the refrigerator, covered, for a couple of hours.

When you are ready to cook the crêpes, add a little oil to a well-seasoned pan set over medium-high heat. Pour about 4 ounces of batter into the hot pan and swirl the pan around to spread the batter thin. Cook until the underside is golden brown and can be lifted without tearing. Turn over and cook on the other side for about a minute. Remove from the pan, spread a couple of teaspoons of Nutella onto the crêpe, and fold it over. Dust with a bit of powdered sugar. Repeat with the rest of the batter.

YIELD: 6 TO 8 (8-INCH) CRÊPES

Dessert **135**

Cake Batter Ice Cream®

Having worked at an ice cream place when I was a teenager, I have never been overly fond of ice cream. With one major exception: Cold Stone Creamery's Cake Batter ice cream. Hands down, this is my favorite flavor of ice cream. Growing up, I loved to lick the batters when my mother baked cakes. This recipe brings back those treasured memories.

3 cups heavy cream, divided

¼ teaspoon salt

¾ cup sugar

½ cup dry Duncan Hines Butter Recipe Cake Mix

1 cup milk

In a heavy stockpot, mix 1 cup of the cream with the salt and sugar. Heat over medium heat, stirring occasionally. When the sugar is completely dissolved, turn off the burner and whisk in the dry cake mix. Add the remaining 2 cups cream and the milk and mix well. Transfer the mixture to a container, cover, and refrigerate for at least 4 hours or overnight.

Whisk the chilled ice cream mixture well—it will be a little lumpy. Freeze in an ice cream maker according to the manufacturer's directions. I like to transfer my ice cream to the freezer to set up for a few hours before serving.

YIELD: 1 QUART

CopyKat.com's **CRACKER BARREL OLD COUNTRY STORE®**

Chocolate Pecan Pie

Chocolate pecan pie is a seasonal favorite at Cracker Barrel Old Country Store during the winter holidays. If you love chocolate and you love pecan pie, you've met your match. Don't worry that the pecans aren't at the top of your pie when you place it in the oven. They'll float upward as the pie cooks. Serve this pie with scoops of ice cream, if you wish.

3 eggs	¼ cup margarine, melted
½ cup sugar	1 cup whole pecans
1 cup light corn syrup	3 tablespoons semisweet chocolate chips
½ teaspoon salt	
1 teaspoons vanilla extract	9-inch unbaked pastry shell

Preheat the oven to 350°F. Beat the eggs in a medium bowl and then add the sugar, mixing well. Mix in the corn syrup, salt, vanilla, and melted margarine. Sprinkle the pecans and chocolate chips into the pie shell. Pour in the filling mixture. The pecans will rise up to the top while the pie is baking. Bake for 50 to 60 minutes, until browned and the filling barely moves when jiggled.

I like to keep this pie in the refrigerator between servings—I think it helps it to set up better.

YIELD: 8 SERVINGS

Pumpkin Custard N' Ginger Snap

Cracker Barrel's Pumpkin Custard N' Ginger Snap dessert is one of their delicious fall recipes. It's hard to resist this creamy, smooth, pumpkin-infused custard.

8 egg yolks

1 (15-ounce) can pure pumpkin

½ cup plus 1 tablespoon sugar, divided*

2¾ cups heavy cream, divided

2 teaspoons pumpkin pie spice, divided

1 teaspoon vanilla extract

1 cup gingersnap cookie crumbs and 8 whole gingersnap cookies

1 tablespoon butter, melted

If you have it, superfine sugar is best to use for the 1 tablespoon that sweetens the whipped cream.

Preheat the oven to 350°F. In a medium glass bowl, whisk the egg yolks until they are creamy and light yellow in color. Add the pumpkin, ½ cup sugar, 1¾ cups cream, 1½ teaspoons pumpkin pie spice, and vanilla; mix until everything is incorporated. Cook this mixture in a double boiler over simmering water, stirring, until it has thickened and a spoon inserted into the custard remains coated when you lift it out. Pour the custard into either 8 individual buttered custard dishes or an 8 x 8-inch buttered baking dish. Bake for 30 to 35 minutes, or until a knife inserted near the center comes out clean. If you are using individual custard dishes, check at 20 to 25 minutes.

While the custard is baking, combine the 1 cup gingersnaps and 1 tablespoon melted butter in a small bowl. Halfway through the baking time, remove the custard(s) from the oven and sprinkle the crumb mixture on top, then finish baking. Let cool to room temperature.

Just before serving, make pumpkin pie spice–infused whipped cream by beating the remaining 1 cup cream with 1 tablespoon sugar and ½ teaspoon pumpkin pie spice until it holds soft peaks. Top the each serving of custard with whipped cream.

∞∞∞∞∞∞∞∞∞∞∞∞∞∞∞∞∞∞∞∞∞
YIELD: 8 SERVINGS

Banana Split Blizzard®

During high school and college I worked at the Dairy Queen. I made more Blizzards during those years than I care to remember. The Banana Split Blizzard is one of my favorites—it has all of the same goodies as a banana split, but it comes in a convenient cup. While DQ Blizzards are made with soft serve ice cream, you can use regular ice cream if you let it soften a little.

2 cups softened vanilla ice cream

3 or 4 banana slices

2 teaspoons chocolate syrup

2 teaspoons pineapple topping

2 teaspoons strawberry topping

2 teaspoons chopped pecans

Place all the ingredients in a blender container and blend for 20 to 30 seconds. Pour into a glass and serve.

YIELD: 1 LARGE BLIZZARD

Chocolate Covered Cherry Blizzard®

The chocolate covered cherry blizzard, or at least that's what they called them when I worked there many years ago, is one of my favorites. Cherry ice cream topping and magic shell topping make up this fun blizzard. If you do not like cherries, you can leave them out, and make a chocolate chip blizzard.

2 cups softened vanilla ice cream

2 teaspoons cherry ice cream topping

2 teaspoons melted Magic Shell (recipe on page 193)

Place all the ingredients in a blender container and blend for 20 to 30 seconds. Pour into a glass and serve.

YIELD: 1 LARGE BLIZZARD

Peanut Butter Parfait Bar

When I worked at Dairy Queen in high school, I made endless parfait bars. Whenever we were standing around, we made these. If you have never tried one, I think you'll agree that the creamy hot chocolate and the salty peanuts go together very well.

1 pint vanilla ice cream

½ cup salted peanuts

½ cup cold hot fudge sauce

6 ounces semisweet chocolate

1 tablespoon coconut oil

6 (3-ounce) Dixie cups

6 Popsicle sticks (craft sticks)

Allow the ice cream to soften. Place about 1 teaspoon peanuts in the bottom of each Dixie cup; follow with about 1 teaspoon hot fudge sauce and then 1 tablespoon ice cream. Repeat with another layer of peanuts, hot fudge, and ice cream, and finish with a layer of peanuts and hot fudge. Insert a Popsicle stick in each cup and freeze for 8 to 10 hours.

Prepare the chocolate coating by melting the semisweet chocolate, in a saucepan over low heat and then stirring in the coconut oil. Peel the paper cup off a frozen ice cream parfait and dip the bar in the melted chocolate, turning to coat; the chocolate will harden. Repeat to coat all the bars. Store in the freezer until ready to enjoy.

YIELD: 6 SERVINGS

Turtlette Blizzard®

I don't know how many different types of Dairy Queen Blizzards there are. I'm certain that there are over 50 or more. Turtle candies are loved by most everyone, so why not prepare a turtle-inspired Blizzard?

2 cups softened ice cream

2 teaspoons butterscotch topping

2 teaspoons melted Magic Shell (recipe on page 193)

2 teaspoons chopped pecans

Place all the ingredients in a blender container and blend for 20 to 30 seconds. Pour into a glass and serve.

◇◇◇◇◇◇◇◇◇◇◇◇◇◇◇◇◇◇◇◇◇◇◇◇◇
YIELD: 1 SERVING

CopyKat.com's DENNY'S®

Maple Bacon Sundae

Let me just say that yes, bacon does taste pretty good on ice cream. Please, before you declare that only someone with Bacon as his middle name would like this sundae, give it a try. While Denny's may not use real maple syrup for their version, you can do so at home if you wish. I've also tried this with butter pecan syrup, and that's also good. PS: My middle name isn't Bacon.

2 strips bacon

2 scoops vanilla ice cream

¼ cup maple-flavored syrup

Cook the bacon very crisp. I prefer to bake my bacon. Baking it means you have no grease splatter in your kitchen, and the pieces cook uniformly. Drain on paper towels and chop into small pieces.

If you have an ice cream sundae glass, place 1 scoop of ice cream in the bottom and add 1 tablespoon maple syrup. Then top with an additional scoop of ice cream, pour in the remaining syrup, and top with the crispy chopped bacon. (If you don't have a fancy sundae glass, you can just place 2 scoops of ice cream in a bowl, add the syrup, and top with the bacon.)

YIELD: 1 SERVING

TIP: I was really prepared not to like this sundae, but I did. We've been combining sweet syrups with our ice cream forever, and salt and sweet just seem to go together. I will say that in playing around with the recipe, I found that using butter pecan syrup instead of the maple-flavored syrup makes it taste extra good.

Red Velvet Pancake Puppies® with Cream Cheese Icing

Denny's has a creative menu that changes often. They've reinvented regular pancake puppies as these warm, tender red velvet puppies, served with a luscious cream cheese dipping sauce.

4 cups vegetable oil, for frying

1 (18¼-ounce) box Duncan Hines Red Velvet cake mix

3 eggs

1 cup water

½ cup white chocolate chips

½ cup (1 stick) butter, at room temperature

1 (8-ounce) package cream cheese, at room temperature

2 cups powdered sugar

½ teaspoon vanilla extract

½ teaspoon lemon extract

1 tablespoon milk

Preheat the oil to 350°F in a deep fryer or a medium saucepan. Using a blender, mix the cake mix and eggs until the batter has no lumps. Stir in the white chocolate chips, using a spoon. Use a 1-ounce cookie scoop to drop batter into the hot oil. Fry on one side for about 1 minute and then flip over and fry on other side for about 1 minute. Drain on a paper towel–lined plate.

Make the cream cheese dipping sauce by beating together the butter and cream cheese until light and fluffy, using an electric mixer. Beat in approximately ½ cup of the powdered sugar. Once that has been incorporated, add the remaining powdered sugar in two more increments. Blend in the vanilla, lemon extract, and milk. Transfer the dipping sauce to a small bowl and serve along with the warm red velvet puppies.

YIELD: 8 TO 10 PUPPIES

TIP: The cooking oil won't be usable for anything else after you make these red velvet puppies, since it will turn red—so fry something else in it first and finish up with these.

CopyKat.com's **EL CHICO CAFÉ®**

Fried Ice Cream

Never had fried ice cream? Let me clear up one thing: we aren't going to just plop ice cream into hot oil. We're going to freeze scoops of ice cream, coat them with corn flakes, freeze them again, and finally give those coated ice cream scoops a quick fry. Then we're going to drizzle them with chocolate sauce and honey. In other words, you need to be patient and plan ahead. I promise that the results will be fantastic—and everyone will be amazed that you can fry ice cream.

1 quart vanilla ice cream	1 beaten egg, beaten
1 cup all-purpose flour	vegetable oil, for frying
1½ cups crushed corn flakes	honey or chocolate syrup
½ cup sugar	whipped cream
½ teaspoon ground cinnamon	maraschino cherries

Starting 8 hours in advance, line a baking sheet with parchment paper or aluminum foil and place in the freezer. Chill for about 30 minutes. Scoop the ice cream into balls and place them on the chilled baking sheet. Freeze for 2 hours.

Place the flour in one small bowl and the beaten egg in another. In a third bowl, mix the crushed corn flakes, sugar, and cinnamon. Roll each ice cream ball with flour, then dip in the egg, and finally coat with the corn flake mixture. Wrap each ice cream ball tightly with plastic wrap. Return the balls to the freezer for another 5 hours.

Pour oil into a deep fryer or saucepan to a depth of 3 to 4 inches, and heat the oil to 450°F. Unwrap each ball and fry in the hot oil very briefly, about 2 seconds. Place in a dessert dish and decorate with toppings, such as honey or chocolate syrup, whipped cream, and a cherry. Serve immediately.

YIELD: 4 TO 6 SERVINGS

Butter Chess Pie

Chess pie is a wonderful old-fashioned dessert that is easy to make. You can even use a prepackaged pie shell from the grocery store; I think the ones in the refrigerated section of the store are fantastic. Buttermilk makes the filling pleasantly tangy. This pie develops an almost crunchy top.

6 tablespoons butter, melted

2 cups sugar

3 tablespoons all-purpose flour

3 large eggs, beaten

1 cup buttermilk

1 teaspoon vanilla extract

¼ teaspoon salt

1 unbaked 9-inch pie shell

Preheat the oven to 350°F. In a medium bowl, combine melted butter, sugar, flour, eggs, buttermilk, vanilla, and salt. Mix well, and pour the filling into the pie shell. Bake for 45 minutes, or until the top begins to turn golden brown.

YIELD: 8 SERVINGS

Streusel Topped Pumpkin Pie

Every year during the holidays we make a pumpkin pie. Have you ever tried one with a streusel topping? This buttery topping adds something special to the pie. Add this streusel topping to this pie, and you will have an empty pie plate at the end of your holiday meal.

1 (15-ounce) can pure pumpkin	2 large eggs
1 (12-ounce) can evaporated milk	½ teaspoon vanilla extract
1 cup sugar, divided	1 (9-inch) unbaked pie shell
½ teaspoon salt	2 tablespoons all-purpose flour
2½ teaspoons pumpkin pie spice	2 tablespoons cold butter

Preheat the oven to 425°F. In a bowl, mix together the pumpkin, evaporated milk, ¾ cup sugar, salt, pumpkin pie spice, eggs, and vanilla. Blend well and pour into the pie shell. Bake for 15 minutes.

While the pie is baking, make the streusel topping. In a small bowl, use a pastry cutter to blend the remaining ¼ cup sugar, flour, and butter, until it resembles cornmeal. After the pie has baked for 15 minutes, carefully remove it from oven and sprinkle on the streusel topping. Reduce the oven temperature to 350°F and bake for an additional 30 minutes.

YIELD: 8 SERVINGS

CopyKat.com's JELL-O®

Pudding Pops

I grew up in the 1980s, and some of the commercials I remember the most are the ones Bill Cosby did for Jello-O pudding pops. I don't know exactly when these disappeared from the grocery store shelves. I wish I could tell you that the copycat recipe is complex, but it isn't. I do recommend purchasing some sort of Popsicle maker. There are fancy ones that are fairly pricey, such as the Zoku brand, that can make a frozen pop in about seven minutes, whereas the old-time plastic molds take much longer. I think the Zoku version makes a better pudding pop due to the quick freezing process. This doesn't allow long ice crystals to form, so you get a really creamy pop.

1 (4-serving) package instant chocolate pudding

2 cups cold milk

Prepare the pudding according to package directions, using the cold milk. Allow the pudding to set for about 2 minutes and then pour it into molds, following the directions for your Popsicle maker.

YIELD: 6 FROZEN POPS

TIP: Don't have a Popsicle maker? Use old-fashioned disposable drinking cups, such as Dixie cups. Fill them three-fourths of the way full, cover the tops with plastic wrap, and then stick a Popsicle (craft) stick through the plastic wrap into each cup. Freeze for at least 6 to 8 hours before unmolding the pops.

CopyKat.com's HOSTESS®

Ding Dongs®

While Hostess may have gone away, you can still prepare many of their favorite dessert treats. I can honestly say that these will taste better than any you bought in a package. They are made with chocolate cake, then filled with a seven-minute frosting and topped with a lovely chocolate ganache.

CHOCOLATE CAKE:

3 ounces unsweetened chocolate

½ cup (1 stick) unsalted butter

2¼ cups packed light brown sugar

3 large eggs

1½ teaspoons vanilla extract

2¼ cups cake flour

2 teaspoons baking soda

½ teaspoon salt

1 cup sour cream

1 cup boiling water

FILLING:

2 egg whites

1½ cups granulated sugar

5 tablespoons water

1½ teaspoons light corn syrup

1 teaspoon vanilla

CHOCOLATE GANACHE:

12 ounces semisweet chocolate

3 tablespoons coconut oil

TO MAKE THE CHOCOLATE CAKE: Preheat the oven to 350°F. Melt the chocolate in a microwave in a microwave-safe dish for 30 second intervals. Remove the dish from the microwave, stir, and repeat as many times to almost melt the chocolate completely. The residual heat in the dish will allow the chocolate to finish melting. Spray a 9 x 13-inch pan with nonstick spray. To make the cake, cream the butter and brown sugar together until light and fluffy with an electric mixer. Add the eggs, vanilla, and melted chocolate and mix well. In a separate bowl, combine the cake flour, baking soda, and salt, mix well. Add the dry ingredients to the creamed mixture alternately with the sour cream and beat until smooth. Pour in the boiling water and stir with a spoon until well blended. The batter will be very thin. Pour the batter into the prepared pan and bake for 30 minutes, or until a tester inserted into the cake comes out clean. Let cool completely in the pan.

TO MAKE THE FILLING: Combine the egg whites, granulated sugar, water, and corn syrup in the top of a double boiler over simmering water and beat with an electric mixer. Place over low to medium heat and continue beating rapidly for 7 minutes, or until the frosting forms soft peaks. Remove from the heat and beat in the vanilla.

Use a 2½-inch biscuit cutter to cut the cake into rounds. Core out the center of each round, about ¾ inch in diameter, saving a portion to use as a plug. Core the cake only about two-thirds of the way though. Spoon filling into a pastry bag fitted with a piping tip. Squeeze filling into the hole in each cake and cover with a cake plug. Place the filled cakes on a cooling rack set on a baking sheet.

TO MAKE THE CHOCOLATE GANACHE: Melt the 12 ounces of chocolate together with the coconut oil in a double boiler over simmering water. Brush ganache onto the cakes. When the ganache has firmed up, about 30 minutes, turn the cakes over and brush ganache on the uncoated portion.

YIELD: 8 TO 10 CAKES

CopyKat.com's **KATZ'S DELI™**

Cheesecake Shake

As if a piece of cheesecake weren't decadent enough, why don't we put it in a glass with some premium ice cream? Yes, Katz's does just this. At this Houston deli, you can order this shake 24 hours a day. Making your own is perfect for whenever you have a slice of cheesecake left over—while unlikely, it's a great thing to do with cheesecake.

1 (4 to 6-ounce) slice New York–style cheesecake

1 cup premium vanilla ice cream

1 tablespoon milk, if needed

Place the slice of cheesecake in a blender and then add the vanilla ice cream. Purée until well blended. If the ice cream is very thick and hard, you may want to add about a tablespoon of milk to your milkshake.

YIELD: 1 OR 2 SERVINGS

TIP: While this version isn't on the Katz menu, I once put a big spoonful of blueberry pie filling into the blender along with the ice cream and cheesecake. It was fantastic. You may want to try other mix-ins, such as chocolate or cherry pie filling.

CopyKat.com's LUBY'S™

Lemon Ice Box Pie

Luby's is one of my favorite cafeterias. They make everything from scratch. This Lemon Ice Box Pie is especially refreshing in summer—light, fluffy, and so easy to make. It's often served with a fresh berry on top of each slice.

1¾ cups graham cracker crumbs

1 cup sugar, divided

½ cup (1 stick) butter, melted

2 (8-ounce) packages cream cheese, softened to room temperature

1 (14-ounce) can sweetened condensed milk

½ cup freshly squeezed lemon juice

4 egg yolks

2 cups heavy cream

¼ cup superfine sugar

½ teaspoon vanilla extract

Preheat the oven to 350°F. In a medium bowl, combine the graham cracker crumbs, melted butter, and ½ cup of the sugar. Blend well and press into a 9-inch pie plate, pressing it into the bottom and all the way up the sides. Bake for 10 minutes.

In a medium bowl, combine the cream cheese, sweetened condensed milk, lemon juice, egg yolks, and remaining ½ cup sugar. Cream together with an electric mixer until the mixture is smooth and creamy. Pour the filling into the pie shell and bake for 25 minutes. Then transfer the pie, uncovered, to the refrigerator and allow it to set up; it will take about 2 hours.

To make the whipped topping, combine the cream, superfine sugar, and vanilla in a bowl. Whip until stiff peaks form. Spoon over the cold pie filling, smoothing the top.

YIELD: 8 SERVINGS

Pecan Pie

Even if you're an inexperienced baker, if you can follow directions and measure, then you can make a pecan pie that's as good as anyone else's. Pecan pie, in my opinion is the easiest pie to make. Just measure everything out, give it a quick stir, and place in the oven, and you'll have a pie that you can brag about.

1 unbaked 9-inch pie shell

1 cup light corn syrup

1 cup sugar

3 large eggs

3 tablespoons butter, melted

1 teaspoon vanilla extract

½ teaspoon salt

1 cup whole pecans

whipped cream, for serving (optional)

Preheat the oven to 350°F. In a medium bowl, combine the corn syrup, sugar, eggs, melted butter, vanilla, and salt, mixing well so the mixture is smooth. Distribute the pecans in the pie shell and pour the corn syrup mixture over them. The pecans will float to the top as the pie cooks. Bake for approximately 1 hour, or until the center is set. Let cool on a wire rack. Serve with whipped cream, if desired.

YIELD: 8 SERVINGS

CopyKat.com's MCDONALD'S®

Eggnog Shake

Many of our favorite restaurants have holiday recipes to help ring in the season, and McDonald's is no exception. The Eggnog Shake on their seasonal menu is made with premium ice cream and is topped with real whipped cream and even a maraschino cherry.

1½ cups premium vanilla ice cream

¾ cup eggnog

whipped cream

maraschino cherry

freshly grated nutmeg (optional)

Using a blender, combine the ice cream and eggnog. Blend until the mixture is smooth and creamy. Pour the shake into a tall glass and top with whipped cream and a cherry. For an extra-special taste, garnish with a sprinkling of freshly ground nutmeg.

YIELD: 1 LARGE SERVING

CopyKat.com's OLIVE GARDEN®

Pumpkin Cheesecake

Love cheesecake and pumpkin pie? With this pumpkin cheesecake, everyone is going to be happy. The cheesecake is sandwiched between a gingersnap cookie crust and a creamy layer of sweetened sour cream. Allow extra time for making the filling, in order to drain the excess moisture from the pumpkin.

CRUST:

1½ cups graham cracker crumbs

1 cup gingersnap cookie crumbs

¼ cup sugar

½ teaspoon ground cinnamon

½ cup (1 stick) butter, melted

CHEESECAKE FILLING:

1 (15-ounce) can pure pumpkin

3 (8-ounce) packages cream cheese

3 eggs

⅔ cup packed light brown sugar

1 teaspoon vanilla extract

½ teaspoon salt

½ teaspoon ground cinnamon

½ teaspoon grated nutmeg

¼ teaspoon ground ginger

¼ teaspoon ground cloves

SOUR CREAM LAYER:

1 cup sour cream

¼ cup sugar

1 teaspoon vanilla extract

⅛ teaspoon ground cinnamon

⅛ teaspoon grated nutmeg (freshly grated, if available)

WHIPPED CREAM AND TOPPINGS:

4 cups heavy cream

¼ cup sugar

½ teaspoon vanilla extract

caramel sauce

gingersnap crumbs

TO MAKE THE CRUST: In a medium bowl, stir together the graham cracker crumbs, gingersnap crumbs, ¼ cup sugar, ½ teaspoon cinnamon, and melted butter; mix well. Press the crust into an 8-inch springform pan, pressing it about halfway up the sides. Refrigerate while you continue to prepare the cheesecake.

TO MAKE THE CHEESECAKE FILLING: Remove the pumpkin from the can and place on a couple of large paper towels. Wrap the pumpkin with the paper towels to help soak up the excess liquid in the purée; set the wrapped pumpkin in a colander nested in a bowl to catch the liquid. Continue to drain excess water from the pumpkin for about 60 minutes. Meanwhile, bring the cream cheese and eggs to room temperature.

Preheat the oven to 350°F. Using an electric mixer, beat the cream cheese until smooth; beat in the eggs, one at a time, and then add the brown sugar, vanilla, salt, cinnamon, nutmeg, ginger, cloves, and drained pumpkin. Beat until very smooth.

Remove the crust from the refrigerator and pour in the filling. Bake for 30 minutes; reduce the oven temperature to 325°F and bake for an additional 30 minutes. The cheesecake should still be slightly jiggly in the center (it will set up nicely as it cools). Remove from the oven.

TO MAKE THE SOUR CREAM LAYER: While the cheesecake bakes, prepare the sour cream layer. In a small bowl, combine the sour cream, sugar, vanilla, cinnamon, and nutmeg. Blend well and spread evenly over the baked cheesecake while it is still warm. Return the cheesecake to the 325°F oven for about 8 minutes, or until the sour cream layer is set. Set on a wire rack and let cool completely.

FOR TOPPINGS: When the cheesecake is completely cool, you can add the whipped cream. In a medium bowl, combine the cream, sugar, and vanilla; whip using a stand mixer or a blender until stiff peaks form. Remove the outer ring from the springform pan and either pipe the whipped cream over the pumpkin cheesecake or spread it on with a knife.

To serve your Olive Garden Pumpkin Cheesecake, drizzle each slice with caramel sauce and sprinkle with gingersnap crumbs.

YIELD: 10 TO 12 SERVINGS

TIP: I don't use a water bath when I make cheesecake. I do have a clay baking stone in my oven, and my cheesecakes turn out very well. You may wish to use a water bath when you prepare your cheesecake. Set the springform pan into a larger pan filled with water. The springform pan should be wrapped with foil to make certain no water from the water ball seeps into the cheesecake while baking.

Original Chocolate Fondue

The Melting Pot is a special-occasion restaurant that serves almost everything fondue style. The service is impeccable, and it doesn't get better than dipping goodies into a warm pot of chocolate. The restaurant serves their fondue with bananas, strawberries, red velvet cake, cheesecake, and marshmallows. You can serve yours with whatever you like. If you don't have a fondue pot, don't let that stop you. You can fashion your own fondue pot by using a double boiler.

8 ounces milk chocolate

3 tablespoons heavy cream

1 tablespoon crunchy peanut butter

dunkers, such as banana slices, strawberries, cubes of red velvet or pound cake, or large marshmallows

In your fondue pot or in a double boiler over simmering water, combine the chocolate and cream. Heat and stir until the cream is fully blended into the chocolate. When you are ready to serve, drop the peanut butter into the pot. Spear your dunking choices with either a fondue fork or a regular fork to dip them into the chocolate. You can either stir the peanut butter completely into the chocolate, or leave as is so you can get a larger scoop of the peanut butter when you dip your favorites into the melted fondue.

YIELD: 2 OR 3 SERVINGS

TIP: This is very good made with dark chocolate, too. You could also swap the crunchy peanut butter for creamy if you prefer.

CopyKat.com's

Peppermint Patties

When I was a child, they aired commercials showing how one bite into a peppermint patty could take you away to a cold place. I love to store these in the refrigerator so that when you bite into one it is literally chilled. I highly recommend using peppermint oil for this recipe rather than peppermint extract. You can find food-grade peppermint oil in many health-food stores and online.

- 2¼ cups powdered sugar, plus more for dusting
- 2 tablespoons butter, at room temperature
- 2 tablespoons evaporated milk

- 1½ teaspoons peppermint oil
- ¼ teaspoon vanilla extract
- 8 ounces semisweet chocolate
- 2 teaspoons coconut oil (or you can substitute vegetable shortening)

Using an electric mixer, blend together the powdered sugar, butter, evaporated milk, peppermint oil, and vanilla. When the mixture forms a uniform ball, cover it with plastic wrap and refrigerate for 20 to 30 minutes. Line a baking sheet with waxed paper and dust with powdered sugar.

Remove the chilled mixture from the refrigerator and use a small melon baller or cookie scoop to form portions of the candy. Roll into small balls and place on the prepared baking sheet. Flatten the balls into flat disks, using the bottom of a drinking glass. Refrigerate for several hours.

Melt the chocolate and coconut oil together in a double boiler over simmering water on the stove. When melted completely, remove from the stove. Gently dip the each peppermint patty in the chocolate, coating both sides, and place back on the waxed paper. Allow the candies to dry completely and become firm before storing; this should take about 30 minutes in the refrigerator, or about 90 minutes at room temperature.

YIELD: 60 PATTIES

TIP: I love to make these candies with the darkest chocolate I can find—at least 60% cacao. For the holiday season, you could sprinkle the tops with nonpareils or other candies while the chocolate is still wet.

Buttercream Icing

For years on my website, people requested Publix Buttercream Icing, and I know that when I receive multiple requests, I have to give that recipe a try. this special icing has a lovely butter and almond flavor that's wonderfully complex. It's also very god for decorating and can hold up to a little bit of heat because the meringue powder helps keep the icing firm.

1 cup (2 sticks) butter, softened

2 cups vegetable shortening, like Crisco

¼ teaspoon salt

1 teaspoon vanilla extract

1 teaspoon butter flavoring*

½ teaspoon almond extract

1 tablespoon meringue powder*

2 pounds powdered sugar

1 tablespoon milk, if needed

Butter flavoring and meringue powder can be found where cake-decorating supplies are sold. This recipe can be made without these ingredients, but the icing tastes better if you use the butter flavoring, and it will hold its shape better with the meringue powder.

Using an electric mixer, mix the butter, shortening, and salt on low speed for 5 minutes. Add the vanilla, butter flavoring, and almond extract; beat until well blended. Turn off the mixer and add the meringue powder and half the powdered sugar to the mixer bowl. Turn the mixer back on at its slowest speed and add the rest of the powdered sugar, ½ cup at a time, until all of it is mixed in. Increase to medium speed and beat until smooth and creamy, about 5 minutes more. If the icing is too thick, add the milk and beat until combined.

YIELD: FROSTING FOR 1 (9-INCH) ROUND DOUBLE-LAYER CAKE

TIP: I highly recommend sifting your powdered sugar before using it in this frosting. Sifting eliminates those clumps that sometimes form in the sugar, making it blend together better. If you don't have a sifter, a regular colander or mesh strainer works well.

Sopapillas

I have to be honest here: I never really thought about Taco Cabana when it came to dessert. But one of my closest friends told me I needed to try their sopapillas. She was dead on—they were fantastic. What makes them so good? You get both honey and dulce de leche to dip them in. Dulce de leche is, well, basically milk jam: milk simmered with sugar until it reduces and turns into a wonderfully thick and creamy sauce. One warning: these are quite addictive.

4 cup all-purpose flour, plus more for rolling

1¼ teaspoons salt

3 teaspoons baking powder

3 tablespoons sugar

2 tablespoons vegetable shortening

1¼ cups milk, or as needed

vegetable shortening, like Crisco, for frying

sugar and ground cinnamon, for sprinkling (optional)

honey

DULCE DE LECHE:

1 (14-ounce) can sweetened condensed milk, such as Eagle Brand

Sift the flour, measure, and sift again into a bowl with the salt, baking powder, and sugar. Cut in the shortening and enough add milk to make a soft dough that's just firm enough to roll. Cover the and let sit for 30 to 60 minutes; then, working on a lightly floured surface, roll the dough to a ¼-inch thickness. Use a sharp knife to cut into diamond-shaped pieces that are 2 x 3 inches.

In a skillet, heat about 1 inch of oil to about 375°F. Add just a few dough pieces to the hot oil at a time (so you don't cool the oil too quickly); turn the pieces at once so they will puff evenly, then turn back to brown both sides. Drain on paper towels and sprinkle with sugar and cinnamon, if you wish. Serve warm with honey and dulce de leche.

FOR THE DULCE DE LECHE: Preheat the oven to 425°F. Pour the sweetened condensed milk into a small ovenproof dish, and place that dish in a 9 x 13-inch baking pan. Fill the 9 x 13 inch baking pan halfway full with water and place in the oven. Check the baking pan ever 30 minutes to ensure that there is water in the pan. Bake for 60 to 90 minutes, depending on how dark you'd like it; the dulce de leche at Taco Cabana is very pale, but you can let yours cook until it has reached a darker shade. Cool before serving. Store left over dulce de leche in an airtight container in the refrigerator. It's also a wonderful addition to coffee.

YIELD: 4 DOZEN SOPAPILLAS (OR MORE)

CopyKat.com's TED'S MONTANA GRILL®

Strawberry Shortcake

I happened into a Ted's Montana Grill on a trip, and I've been wishing ever since that one would open in my town. Their strawberry shortcake is the old-fashioned kind—no sponge cake, but a sweet cream biscuit for your strawberries to rest upon. Topped with ice cream and whipped cream, this will have you wishing that strawberry season would last forever.

1 pound strawberries, sliced (about 3 cups)

1½ tablespoons sugar, plus more for the biscuit tops

2 cups all-purpose flour

2½ teaspoons baking powder

½ teaspoon salt

1¼ cups heavy cream

4 scoops Häagen-Dazs or other premium vanilla ice cream

whipped cream, for topping

Place the strawberries a container with a lid, and sprinkle the 1½ tablespoons sugar over them. Cover and let macerate for a couple of hours before using.

Preheat the oven to 450°F. Grease a baking sheet. Sift together the flour, baking powder, and salt. Mix in the cream until the flour is just incorporated. Gently knead the dough on a floured surface and shape into 4 biscuits at least ½ to ¾ inch thick. Place on the prepared baking sheet. Sprinkle the tops with sugar. Bake for 10 to 15 minutes, until the biscuits are golden brown.

To assemble the shortcakes, slice each biscuit in half and lay the bottom half on a plate. Add a scoop of ice cream and a generous spoonful of strawberries, then top with the other half of the biscuit and whipped cream. Spoon additional strawberries around the biscuit.

YIELD: 4 SERVINGS

TIP: This is a great make-ahead dessert. Bake the biscuits and macerate the strawberries in advance, and then assemble the shortcakes right before serving. Add blackberries or blueberries to the mixture for a wonderful new creation. If you have sugar with larger crystals, this is ideal for sprinkling on top of the biscuits before they bake.

Vanilla Bean Cheesecake

When something has been on the menu for years, and I mean *years*, it has to be good. This vanilla bean cheesecake requires an extra step or two, but it is so worth it! Everyone will wonder how you made something that tastes this good.

CRUST:

1½ cups graham cracker crumbs

3 tablespoons sugar

6 tablespoons butter, melted

¼ teaspoon ground cinnamon

CHEESECAKE FILLING:

3 (8-ounce) packages cream cheese

1⅓ cups sugar

5 large eggs

1 teaspoon vanilla extract

1 vanilla bean

2 teaspoons freshly squeezed lemon juice

¼ cup all-purpose flour

2 cups sour cream

WHITE CHOCOLATE MOUSSE:

4 egg yolks

¼ cup sugar

2½ cups heavy cream, divided

1 cup (6 ounces) white chocolate chips*

1 vanilla bean

white chocolate curls (optional)

* *I really like Ghirardelli white chocolate chips; I find they have excellent flavor.*

TO MAKE THE CRUST: In a bowl, stir together the graham cracker crumbs, sugar, cinnamon, and melted butter. Press the crust into a 9-inch springform pan. Refrigerate until time to bake. If you want a firm crust, you can bake it for 10 minutes at 350°F before filling.

FOR FILLING: Allow all the cheesecake filling ingredients to warm to room temperature. Preheat the oven to 325°F.

In a large bowl, combine the cream cheese, sugar, and eggs. Blend with an electric mixer until smooth and creamy. Add the vanilla extract and the seeds scraped from 1 vanilla pod along with the lemon juice, flour, and sour cream. Blend until smooth and velvety. Pour the filling over the crust in the springform pan and place in the oven. After 45 minutes, begin checking every 5 minutes for doneness. The cheesecake will be done when the outer edges are firm but the middle is slightly wet-looking and jiggles when the pan is gently shaken. Transfer the cheesecake to a wire rack and let cool completely to room temperature before placing it in the refrigerator. Ideally, it should be refrigerated overnight before the white chocolate mousse is added.

TO MAKE THE WHITE CHOCOLATE MOUSSE: Beat the egg yolks with an electric mixer on high for 2 to 3 minutes, or until they are thick, foamy, and light yellow. Beat in the sugar until combined. Heat 1 cup heavy cream in a medium saucepan over medium-low heat until just hot. Gradually stir half of the hot cream into the yolks, stirring rapidly so you don't end up with scrambled eggs. Return the egg mixture to the saucepan with the hot cream and cook on low for about 5 minutes, stirring, until thickened. Stir in the white chocolate chips and let them melt. Cover and refrigerate for about 2 hours.

Beat the remaining 1½ cups heavy cream until soft peaks form and add the seeds scraped from the vanilla bean. Fold in the refrigerated white chocolate mixture and spoon onto the top of the chilled cheesecake. It is not necessary to chill the mousse before adding to the cheesecake layer.

If you wish, you can decorate the white chocolate mouse with white chocolate curls. Make the curls by scraping a vegetable peeler across a block of white chocolate. Sprinkle them over the top of the cheesecake.

YIELD: 16 SERVINGS

TIP: When preparing a cheesecake, have all the ingredients at room temperature before you start. Use only full-fat cream cheese for this recipe, not light cream cheese. The full-fat cream cheese and the ingredients at room temperature help prevent the cheesecake from cracking. The fat from the cream cheese makes the batter more resilient and the ingredients at room temperature keep the batter from being shocked from the change in temperature. This will help cracks from forming. Cheesecakes are very sensitive to heat. Ovens are different and can be temperamental, but you can overcome their shortcomings by purchasing an oven thermometer.

Breakfast

Maybe you eat breakfast out when you travel, or perhaps you go out for breakfast on the weekend. Breakfast is the one meal that I love to eat out, but sometimes restaurants are really busy then and I don't want to wait 45 minutes—so I whip up a wonderful breakfast at home.

I'll show you how to make sawmill gravy like the Cracker Barrel does—great for biscuits and toast. You'll learn how to make many kinds of pancakes, just like IHOP does; your family will be amazed when you make Cinn-a-Stack and pumpkin pancakes. You can continue to amaze them with the only breakfast appetizer I know of, Denny's famous pancake puppies.

Don't stress about serving the same old bacon and eggs. Let's turn breakfast into a special meal that everyone will enjoy.

Sawmill Gravy

You know that when you're on the road, you can always get a home-style breakfast at the Cracker Barrel. Their sawmill gravy goes great over their fresh biscuits. While this isn't sausage gravy, we do need just a little bit of sausage for flavor. I like to make this gravy when I'm frying sausage patties, so I can eat the sausage for breakfast.

2 tablespoons butter

2 tablespoons all-purpose flour

2 cups whole milk

½ teaspoon salt

¾ teaspoon ground black pepper

2 teaspoons cooked crumbled sausage

In a medium skillet over medium heat, melt the butter and whisk in the flour. Continue to stir until the mixture has reached the consistency of paste, begins to turn slightly golden brown, and starts to smell like pie crust. Whisk in approximately ½ cup of the milk. Once the milk has thickened, add another ½ cup milk and stir until thickened. Finally add the rest of the milk and stir until it thickens. Reduce the heat to simmer and add the salt, pepper, and crumbled sausage. Simmer on low for 10 minutes; the gravy will reduce in volume. Serve with your favorite biscuits, toast, or even on top of fried potatoes.

YIELDS: 1½ CUPS

CopyKat.com's DENNY'S®

Pancake Puppies®

Denny's is the only place where I know you can get a breakfast "appetizer." Their original pancake puppy was a wonderful cinnamon and sugar version. If you enjoy these, you can pair them with a scoop of vanilla ice cream and add a drizzle of chocolate syrup to make their pancake puppy sundae.

4 cups vegetable oil, for frying

2 cups Krusteaz buttermilk pancake mix

1 cup water

2 tablespoons sugar mixed with 2 teaspoons ground cinnamon

pancake syrup, for serving

Pour the oil into a medium pot or a deep fryer and heat to 350°F. In a bowl, mix together the pancake mix and water.

Use a cookie scoop to scoop out pancake batter and drop it into the hot oil. Turn the pancake puppy when the dough ball turns brown, using a slotted spoon, and cook until the other side has browned, 2 to 3 minutes. Remove from the hot oil and drain on paper towels, then roll in the cinnamon-sugar mixture. Be sure to serve these with plenty of syrup.

YIELD: 4 TO 6 SERVINGS

TIP: If you have leftover cinnamon and sugar, save it to use in oatmeal or sprinkle on toast.

Blueberry and White Chocolate Pancake Puppies®

Since pancake puppies are so popular with Denny's customers, they've also created seasonal ones, like these blueberry and white chocolate puppies. Here I think the Krusteaz mix tastes very good and holds up better in frying than some other grocery store brands.

4 cups vegetable oil for frying

2 cups Krusteaz blueberry pancake mix

1 cup water

⅓ cup white chocolate chips

½ cup powdered sugar

pancake syrup, for serving

Pour the oil into a medium pot or deep fryer and heat to 350°F. In a bowl, combine the pancake mix, water, and white chocolate chips and stir until blended. Use a cookie scoop to scoop out pancake batter and drop it into the hot oil. Turn each pancake puppy over when the dough ball turns brown, using a slotted spoon, and cook until the other side has browned.

Drain the puppies on paper towels and roll them in powdered sugar. Top with any remaining powdered sugar and serve with your favorite pancake syrup.

YIELD: 4 TO 6 SERVINGS

CopyKat.com's **GRAND LUX CAFE®**

Fried Chicken and Waffles

The Grand Lux Cafe—owned by the same people that brought you the Cheesecake Factory—serves a very nice weekend brunch. Included on the menu are some upscale fried chicken and waffles. The chicken is dipped in buttermilk and dredged in seasoned flour before it is fried. The crisp waffles are served with a sweet butter sauce. This recipe makes quite a bit, so invite friends and family. You can amaze them with how well you cook, and they can amaze you with how well they do the dishes.

WAFFLE BATTER:

1½ cups lukewarm water (105 to 110°F)

1 package active dry yeast, or 1 tablespoon dry yeast

⅓ cup plus 1 teaspoon sugar, divided

3 cups sifted all-purpose flour

¼ teaspoon salt

3 large egg yolks

4 large egg whites, divided

1½ cups whole milk

½ cup (1 stick) butter, melted and cooled

2 teaspoons vegetable oil

2 teaspoons vanilla extract

1 teaspoon almond extract

Sweetened Butter Sauce (recipe on page 190)

powdered sugar, for dusting (optional)

CHICKEN TENDERS:

4 cups vegetable shortening, for frying

3 cups all-purpose flour

1½ teaspoons ground black pepper

2 teaspoons seasoned salt

1 teaspoon salt

3 cups buttermilk

2 pounds chicken tenders

FOR WAFFLE BATTER: Dissolve the yeast in lukewarm water (105 to 110°F) with 1 teaspoon sugar. Let stand for 5 to 10 minutes, until the yeast begins to bubble and foam.

In a large bowl, stir the flour with the salt. In a medium bowl, combine the yeast mixture with the 3 egg yolks, 1 egg white, and remaining ⅓ cup sugar; stir to blend. Add the remaining water, milk, melted butter, oil, vanilla, and almond extract; stir until the batter is smooth and creamy. Stir the liquid mixture into the flour mixture and beat until smooth.

Beat the remaining 3 egg whites in a clean, dry bowl. (If the bowl isn't perfectly clean, the whites may not fluff up as much as they can.) Beat until stiff peaks form. Fold the egg whites gently into the batter. Let the batter stand for 1 hour, stirring every 15 minutes.

TO MAKE THE CHICKEN TENDERS: In a deep pot or deep fryer, preheat the vegetable oil to 350°F. In a medium bowl, stir together the flour, pepper, seasoned salt, and salt. Pour the buttermilk into a shallow 8 x 8-inch baking dish. Pat the chicken tenders dry with a paper towel. Dredge each tender in the seasoned flour, shake off the excess, and dip in the buttermilk. Dip back into the seasoned flour, shake off the excess flour, and set aside on a plate. (If you don't shake off the excess flour, it may burn in the hot grease—and that can make the chicken taste burnt.) Let the chicken tenders rest for 5 minutes before cooking so that the crust will form a nice crunchy outer layer.

Fry only a few chicken tenders at a time; this way the oil will stay at the correct temperature. Fry for 5 to 6 minutes, or until golden brown. Depending on the depth of the hot oil you may need to turn over the chicken tenders about 3 minutes into the cooking so they can brown properly. Place on a plate covered with paper towels to drain.

TO ASSEMBLE THE WAFFLES: Preheat a Belgian waffle maker to medium heat. Scoop batter onto the waffle maker; you may want to use a heatproof spatula to spread it evenly over the grids. Close and cook until the waffle is done; most waffle makers have indicators to let you know when the waffle is ready. You can keep your waffles warm in an oven set at 200°F until you are ready to serve them.

To serve, place a waffle on a plate and top with 4 chicken tenders. Dust with powdered sugar, if desired, and the Grand Lux Sweetened Butter Sauce to pour over.

YIELD: 4 SERVINGS

CopyKat.com's IHOP®

Bacon Temptation Omelets

Who doesn't love bacon? Pork belly goes with almost anything. My version of IHOP's Bacon Temptation is likely to make bacon-lovers so happy. This large omelet has *lots* of bacon, a tangy cheese sauce, and shredded cheese. IHOP adds a little pancake batter to their omelets to make them light and fluffy, and you can do the same. If you want to go gluten-free, don't add the pancake mix.

4 ounces American cheese

2 tablespoons milk, divided

4 large eggs

6 slices bacon, cut into small pieces and cooked, divided

2 tablespoons prepared pancake mix

¼ cup shredded Monterey Jack–Colby cheese blend

Preheat a griddle or a skillet to 350°F. In a small saucepan over medium heat, melt the American cheese with 1 tablespoon of the milk, stirring. Reduce the heat to simmer while you prepare the eggs.

In a medium bowl, combine the eggs, bacon pieces from 4 bacon slices, the pancake batter, and the remaining 1 tablespoon milk. Whisk vigorously until all is well blended. Spray the griddle with nonstick spray and pour the omelet mixture over the griddle, using a spatula to maintain a large, rectangular shape. Pour half of the cheese sauce over the top eggs. When the eggs are almost done they will look dry. Roll the omelet into a tight, uniform roll and transfer to a plate. Garnish with the shredded cheese and remaining bacon pieces.

YIELD: 1 SERVING

CopyKat.com's **IHOP®**

Banana Bread French Toast

I think IHOP is known for their creativity when it comes to filling breakfast dishes. Often we have used different breads at home to make cinnamon toast, but who would have thought to use banana bread? Then we're going to top this with caramel sauce, sliced bananas, and a bit of whipped cream. Nothing screams special Sunday breakfast like the IHOP Banana Bread French Toast.

2 large eggs, divided

2 tablespoons milk, divided

4 slices banana bread

1 banana, sliced

4 teaspoons butter

4 tablespoons caramel sauce

whipped cream

freshly grated nutmeg (optional)

In a bowl, whisk together the eggs and the milk. Heat a skillet over medium heat and add 1 teaspoon of butter for each slice of banana bread being cooked in the skillet at one time. Dip each slice of banana bread in the egg mixture to coat evenly; flip the slice over to coat the other side. Cook in the hot skillet for about 1 minute on each side. Place 2 cooked slices on each plate and add half the banana slices. Drizzle with caramel sauce and then top with whipped cream and, if desired, a grating of nutmeg.

YIELD: 2 SERVINGS

Cinn-a-Stack® Pancakes

Leave it to IHOP to offer the taste of a cinnamon roll in a pancake. They even drizzle this with a cream cheese icing, so you can set the pancake syrup aside when you try these rich pancakes. Use any leftover butter spread to make cinnamon toast.

CINNAMON LAYER:

½ cup butter, softened

1 cup packed brown sugar

1 tablespoon ground cinnamon

2 teaspoons cake flour

⅛ teaspoon salt

¼ teaspoon vanilla extract

CREAM CHEESE ICING:

¼ cup (½ stick) butter

4 ounces cream cheese

1 cup powdered sugar

1 tablespoon milk

½ teaspoon vanilla extract

PANCAKES:

1¼ cups all-purpose flour

1½ teaspoons baking powder

2½ teaspoons sugar

½ teaspoon salt

½ teaspoon baking soda

1½ cups buttermilk, plus ⅛ to ¼ cup more if needed to thin the batter

2 tablespoons vegetable oil

1 egg, slightly beaten

TO MAKE THE CINNAMON LAYER: In a small bowl combine the butter, brown sugar, cake flour, cinnamon, salt, and vanilla. Stir until well blended; set aside.

TO MAKE THE CREAM CHEESE ICING: In a blender, first mix the cream cheese and butter until light and fluffy. Slowly add the powdered sugar. When the sugar has been incorporated, blend in the milk and vanilla.

TO MAKE THE PANCAKES: Place the dry pancake ingredients (flour through baking soda) in a bowl and stir to blend. Add 1½ cups buttermilk, oil, and egg. Use a spoon to mix the ingredients and beat until smooth. Heat a skillet or griddle on medium-low heat and spray with nonstick spray, or add a little oil. Pour in about ⅓ cup of batter to form a 4-inch pancake.

When the pancakes start to show small bubbles on top, turn them over to finish cooking. (Turning them is much easier if you spray your pancake turner with nonstick spray.) If the batter seems too thick, add a little more buttermilk; mix well.

You can assemble the stacks as you go, but if you plan on making a few ahead of time, it is best to assemble what you need to serve immediately. To assemble a Cinn-a-Stack, decide how many pancakes you want in the stack and lay the first pancake on a plate. Spread about 2 teaspoons of the cinnamon mixture over the pancake, then add the next pancake and another cinnamon layer. When you are done adding pancakes, top with a final cinnamon layer and drizzle on the cream cheese icing.

YIELD: 10 PANCAKES

CopyKat.com's IHOP®

Pumpkin Spice Pancakes

Often it's the followers of CopyKat.com who have the best ideas for what recipe to tackle next. Before I tried these pancakes, I thought the concept was, quite frankly, a little scary. A few readers suggested it, and since I'm here to deliver what you want, I tried them. You know, I really like these pancakes! They are a perfect fall harvest on a plate, almost creamy, but spiced just like pumpkin pie.

1¼ cups all-purpose flour

1½ teaspoons baking powder

1½ tablespoons sugar

½ teaspoon salt

½ teaspoon baking soda

2 tablespoons vegetable oil, plus more for the pan

1 egg, slightly beaten

1½ cups buttermilk, plus ⅛ to ¼ cup more if needed to thin the batter

⅓ cup puréed pumpkin (pumpkin from a can will work)

1 teaspoon vanilla extract

1½ teaspoons pumpkin pie spice

powdered sugar and whipped cream (optional)

In a medium bowl, use a fork to stir together the flour, baking powder, sugar, salt, and baking soda. Add the vegetable oil, egg, and 1½ cups buttermilk and stir just until well blended. Add the pumpkin, vanilla, and pumpkin pie spice, stirring until you have a uniform mixture.

Heat a skillet over medium heat, or heat a griddle to 350°F. Oil the cooking area slightly with vegetable oil. Pour batter onto the hot surface; I find about ½ cup batter creates a pancake that's easy to handle. When the edges become dry and small bubbles form, flip the pancakes and cook for another minute or two. (These pancakes do take a little longer to cook than other pancakes; the pumpkin seems to slow the cooking process just a bit.)

To serve your pancakes just like IHOP, sprinkle on some powdered sugar and top with whipped cream.

YIELDS: 4 SERVINGS

CopyKat.com's **LA MADELEINE™**

Smart Choice Omelet

Here's a nice and light breakfast that can be prepared quickly and easily. This whole breakfast has fewer than 500 calories, and you even get a slice of bread. Sautéed mushrooms, onions, and spinach turn ordinary Egg Beaters into a special breakfast.

nonstick spray	1 cup Egg Beaters
¼ cup chopped onion	½ cup fresh spinach
¼ cup sliced mushrooms	tomato slices
salt and pepper	2-ounce French baguette piece

Coat an 8-inch nonstick skillet heavily with nonstick spray. Over low heat, cook the onion and mushrooms in the skillet until the onions turn translucent. Season to taste with salt and pepper. Pour the Egg Beaters over the cooked onions and mushrooms and sprinkle with the spinach. Allow the eggs to cook fully, 2 to 3 minutes, and then turn the omelet over on itself and let the spinach steam for a few moments. Serve with fresh tomato slices and a piece of baguette bread.

As written, this recipe is about 350 calories and 8 Weight Watcher Plus Points. You could also use other vegetables, and it would still be a healthy choice for breakfast. Adding cheese and meat, of course, would increase the calories.

YIELD: 1 SERVING

CopyKat.com's **LUBY'S™**

Creamy Grits

Not everyone makes delicious and full-flavored grits, but Luby's make the creamiest grits that you can get in a restaurant. What makes theirs so good? They use milk instead of just water when they cook their grits. Serve up this Southern favorite with a little bit of butter and a sprinkling of salt and pepper.

2 cups whole milk

¾ cup grits (5-minute grits, not instant)

4 teaspoons sugar

1 tablespoon butter

½ teaspoon salt

¼ teaspoon pepper, if desired

Pour the milk into a medium saucepan over medium heat and heat until it simmers. Whisk in the grits and sugar and simmer for about 5 minutes, stirring continually as the grits swell and finish cooking. Stir in the butter. Season with salt and pepper to taste.

YIELD: 4 SERVINGS

Sausage Steak

Sausage topped with crispy bacon, melted cheese, and green onions makes for a hearty breakfast that you can prepare any day of the week.

1 pound ground sausage

½ cup beef broth

½ cup shredded Cheddar cheese

¼ cup thinly sliced green onions

¼ pound bacon, cooked crisp and chopped into small pieces

Divide the ground sausage into 6 patties. Shape the patties into oblongs and place them in a 9 x 13-inch baking dish. Pour in the beef broth. Broil in the oven on high until the sausage is completely cooked through, following the directions for your oven's broiler; this may only take 10 to 13 minutes. Remove from the oven and top with the cheese, green onions, and bacon. Return the sausage steaks to the oven and broil 1 or 2 minutes until the cheese is melted.

YIELD: 6 PATTIES

CopyKat.com's MCDONALD'S®

Egg McMuffin™

This classic breakfast sandwich has been around for as long as I can remember. I love to make several on the weekend so that I can simply reheat and go during the week. I promise that the time you spend making these will be less than what you'd spend in the drive-thru line! When you make these at home, you can substitute Canadian bacon for the sausage in the McDonald's version, or you could use a turkey sausage patty for a lighter alternative.

1 slice Canadian bacon

nonstick spray

1 egg

1 English muffin

½ teaspoon butter

1 slice American cheese (such as Kraft Singles)

In a small skillet, brown the Canadian bacon over medium heat for about 60 seconds on each side. Remove the bacon from the pan and set aside. Coat an egg ring or a canning-jar ring with nonstick spray to use as your egg mold. Set the ring in the hot skillet and crack the egg into the ring. Cook until the egg has set. Gently remove the ring, flip the egg over, and cook on the other side for another 60 seconds. Toast the English muffin and spread ¼ teaspoon butter on each half. Place the cheese slice on the bottom bun and add the ham, then the egg, and finally the top half of the muffin.

YIELD: 1 SANDWICH

TIP: You don't have to use an egg ring or canning jar ring—you can cook your eggs free-form. You may even want to change the cheese to a Swiss cheese. If made ahead, these take about 60 to 90 seconds to reheat in the microwave.

CopyKat.com's STARBUCKS™

Pumpkin Bread

This pumpkin bread—spiced with cinnamon, nutmeg, allspice, and a touch of clove—is so good, and so moist! And you could make many loaves of this tasty bread for what you'd spend on a single loaf from the coffee house.

- nonstick spray
- 1½ cups all-purpose flour
- 1 cup sugar
- ¾ teaspoon salt
- 1 teaspoon baking soda
- ½ teaspoon grated nutmeg
- ¼ teaspoon ground cardamom
- ½ teaspoon ground cinnamon
- ¼ teaspoon ground allspice
- ¼ teaspoon ground cloves
- 2 eggs, beaten
- ½ cup vegetable oil (don't use olive or peanut oil)
- 1 cup pumpkin purée
- ½ teaspoon vanilla extract
- ⅓ to ½ cup roasted and salted pumpkin seeds

Preheat the oven to 350°F. Spray a 9 x 5 x 3-inch loaf pan with nonstick spray. Sift the dry ingredients (flour, sugar, salt, baking soda, and spices) together into a large bowl. In a smaller bowl, combine the eggs, oil, pumpkin, and vanilla, mixing well. Pour the liquid ingredients over the dry ingredients. Stir until there are no lumps, but don't overstir. Pour into the prepared pan and sprinkle the pumpkin seeds on top. Bake for 50 to 60 minutes, or until a toothpick poked into the center comes out clean. Let the bread cool in the pan for about 5 minutes and then turn it out onto a cooling rack. The bread cuts best when allowed to cool completely.

YIELD: 8 SLICES

TIP: If you wish, you can use a scant 2 teaspoons of pumpkin pie spice in place of the spices listed in the ingredients.

Ultimate Meat & Cheese™ Breakfast Burrito

I don't know what it is about breakfast burritos, but they're so satisfying. I can't think of a better breakfast invention. I love Sonic for their breakfast and their unique drinks. I've always harbored a secret wish to create a blog that pairs food with their more than six million drink combinations—but that's for another day and another book.

nonstick spray

1½ cups frozen Tater Tots

1 pound ground sausage

½ pound bacon

6 ounces American cheese (you can use single cheese slices)

4 tablespoons milk, divided

10 eggs

salt and pepper

½ cup shredded Cheddar cheese

jalapeño pepper slices (optional)

Preheat the oven to 350°F. Spay a baking sheet with nonstick spray and place the Tater Tots on the baking sheet. Bake for approximately 22 to 25 minutes. (Or you can deep-fry the tater tots if you like them extra crispy.)

While the tots are in the oven, cook the sausage in a skillet over medium heat until it is well browned. Drain over paper towels and cover with another paper towel to help keep the heat in. In the same pan, cook the bacon until crispy. Drain on paper towels.

Prepare the cheese sauce by heating together the cheese and 2 tablespoons milk in a small saucepan over medium heat, stirring until the cheese is fully melted and the mixture has a uniform texture. Turn off the burner but leave the pot on the burner so that the residual heat will keep the sauce warm.

In a medium bowl, whisk the eggs together with the remaining 2 tablespoons milk. Spray a skillet with nonstick spray and heat over medium heat. Pour in the eggs, season with salt and pepper, and stir gently until the eggs have cooked.

Heat the tortillas in the microwave for about 60 seconds to make them warm and pliable. Assemble your breakfast burritos by distributing the eggs, sausage, Tater Tots, bacon, and cheese sauce over the tortillas. I also like to add a couple of jalapeños to mine, but that is a personal choice. Sprinkle with the shredded Cheddar, wrap up burrito-style, and serve.

YIELD: 6 SERVINGS

CopyKat.com's **WHATABURGER®**

Breakfast on a Bun®

Whataburger is one of my favorite places to get breakfast. What I like the most is that your food is made fresh to order, which means you always get a piping-hot meal.

2 slices bacon (or 1 sausage patty)

1 egg

1 small hamburger bun

1 slice American cheese

Set a skillet over medium heat and cook the bacon in the skillet. Once the bacon has started to release some of its grease, place a wide-mouth canning ring in the skillet alongside the bacon. Crack the egg inside the ring. Remove the bacon when it is done and drain on paper towels. Turn the egg over and to cook the other side; it should take about 30 seconds once you've flipped it over. (The Whataburger sandwiches are served with solid, not runny, yolks.)

To assemble the sandwich, place the bacon on the bottom half of the bun, breaking it in half to fit if needed. Add the egg and then the cheese. Place the top bun on the cheese.

YIELD: 1 SANDWICH

Bacon, Egg, and Cheese Taquito

I moved away from Texas for a few months in 2008, though I quickly came back when I realized there is lots of snow in other places. One thing I really missed was breakfast taquitos from Whataburger. A griddle is an easy way to prepare the whole taquito, because you can do so much of at once, but otherwise a large skillet will do. You can serve this with your favorite salsa.

2 slices bacon	1 flour tortilla
2 large eggs	salt and pepper
2 teaspoons milk	1 slice American cheese

Preheat a griddle to 350°F. On one side of the griddle, fry the bacon on both sides until crisp. Leave the other side of the griddle clean for the eggs. While the bacon is cooking, in a small bowl whisk together the eggs and milk. When the bacon is done, remove it and wipe off the bacon grease. Heat the tortilla on the grill for about 30 seconds on each side. Spray the clean side of the grill with a little nonstick spray and pour the eggs onto it. Season with salt and pepper. Cook the eggs, gently stirring until done. Build the taquito by placing the cheese on the tortilla, then adding the scrambled eggs and finally the cooked bacon. Fold over the tortilla sides to enclose the filling.

YIELD: 1 TAQUITO

Sauces and Dressings

For me, condiments often are what makes a meal. Could you imagine eating your favorite burger without its special sauce? In this chapter you'll find out how to make sauces for your hamburgers along with all sorts of dipping sauces and dressings.

Balsamic Vinegar Reduction

This is a versatile sauce that can be drizzled over meats, salads, and even ice cream. I have seen bottles of balsamic vinegar reduction sold in stores for quite a lot of money. In fact, I scratch my head and wonder why someone would purchase this when it can be made so easily at home. I buy balsamic vinegar in large bottles from Costco, then simply simmer it to produce a wonderfully thick balsamic vinegar reduction.

2 cups balsamic vinegar

Pour the vinegar into a small nonreactive saucepan and simmer over low heat until it has reduced by half, about 30 minutes. Let cool completely and then store in an airtight container. The vinegar reduction should be used within 60 days. After that, the vinegar begins to crystalize, and while it's still perfectly good to use, it loses the velvety smooth texture it once had. This can be stored either in the refrigerator or at room temperature.

YIELD: APPROXIMATELY 1 CUP

CopyKat.com's

Chinese Hot Mustard

Do you ever wonder why those take-out packets of hot mustard never taste quite the same as the mustard in the restaurant? It's because hot mustard tastes best when it is made fresh. If you are near an Asian store, I highly recommend buying Chinese hot mustard powder. Otherwise, an English mustard such as Colman's will also work very well, so you can always have hot Chinese-style mustard available.

¼ cup dry mustard powder

¼ cup warm water

2 teaspoons vegetable oil

1 teaspoon seasoned rice wine vinegar

Combine all the ingredients in a small bowl and stir to blend. In about 15 minutes, the flavor will fully develop. Consume quickly, since this will lose its heat over time.

YIELD: APPROXIMATELY ⅓ CUP

CopyKat.com's **GRAND LUX CAFE®**

Sweetened Butter

During the weekend brunch at the Grand Lux Cafe, pancakes and waffles come with this sweetened butter. You can easily replicate this decadent treat at home with good-quality butter and powdered sugar.

½ cup (1 stick) butter   1 tablespoon powdered sugar

In a small saucepan over low heat, gently melt the butter. Stir in the powdered sugar. Serve warm. (To keep it warm longer, pour the sweetened butter into a small ceramic container that has been warmed in hot water. That way the container won't draw heat away from the butter, and the butter will remain in a liquid state longer.)

YIELD: 4 SERVINGS

TIP: You could also infuse this butter with a little grated lemon or orange zest. Adding about ⅛ teaspoon grated zest is a very nice touch when serving this with French toast.

CopyKat.com's

Homemade Taco Seasoning

There are many ways to save money at the grocery store, and preparing your own taco seasoning is one of them. Another benefit of this taco seasoning is that it is salt free.

6 teaspoons chili powder

5 teaspoons paprika

4½ teaspoons ground cumin

2½ teaspoons garlic powder

3 teaspoons onion powder

¼ teaspoon cayenne pepper

¼ teaspoon dried oregano

Combine all the ingredients in a small bowl and mix well. Store in an airtight container for up to 6 months. Use 3 tablespoons taco seasoning mix with 1 cup water to season 1 pound of ground beef.

YIELD: SEASONING FOR 3 POUNDS OF GROUND BEEF.

TIP: For a great way to dress up sour cream, add a couple teaspoons of this taco seasoning to 1 cup of sour cream. Serve with tortilla chips for dipping.

CopyKat.com's

Honey Mustard

I've been known to ask for extra condiments at restaurants, but why bother when this is so easy to make? Honestly, I think this homemade honey mustard tastes a little better than what you often get at restaurants. It's a great addition to fried chicken breasts, chicken nuggets, pork chops, and sandwiches. I have even been known to slip some into my homemade deviled eggs.

½ cup mayonnaise

2 tablespoons prepared yellow mustard

1½ tablespoons honey

1 teaspoon seasoned rice wine vinegar

⅛ teaspoon paprika

⅛ teaspoon cayenne pepper

In small bowl, whisk all the ingredients together until well blended. Store in an airtight container in the refrigerator.

YIELD: APPROXIMATELY ¾ CUP

TIP: To turn this honey mustard into salad dressing, thin it with 1 or 2 tablespoons vegetable oil and drizzle over salad greens.

CopyKat.com's

Magic Shell™

Magic Shell is a chocolate sauce that hardens over cold ice cream. In fact, it's what coats the Dairy Queen Peanut Buster Parfait Bars (page 142). Use it on top of your favorite ice cream, or warm it up and drizzle it into a blender with ice cream to make a chocolate chip shake. Coconut oil is commonly found in many grocery stores now. You can also make this with shortening instead, but the coconut oil smells heavenly and is closer to what's served at ice cream parlors all over the world.

12 ounces semisweet chocolate chips

3 tablespoons coconut oil

Gently melt the chocolate in a double boiler over simmering water. Add the coconut oil and stir to blend. You can refrigerate the sauce in a plastic squeeze bottle and then, when you're ready to use it, simply drop the bottle into a large glass of warm water to melt the sauce. I love to pour a little of this into an ice cream cone before loading it full of ice cream.

YIELD: 12 SERVINGS

CopyKat.com's

Simple Syrup

I've seen simple syrup for sale in stores recently. It boggles my mind when we purchase items that are so simple to make at home and literally cost pennies. Simple syrup is an elegant way to sweeten iced tea, coffee, and cocktails. I first encountered it at a very nice restaurant in San Antonio. Las Canarias served a small pitcher of simple syrup with their iced tea. It is simple to make, and with a few additions you can serve your own fancy drinks. Add a touch of vanilla and prepare your own vanilla latte.

2 cups sugar   1 cup warm water

Combine the sugar and water in a small saucepan over medium-low heat until the sugar has dissolved completely. Remove the syrup from the heat and allow it to cool, then transfer it to an airtight container. Sweeten coffee and tea with the simple syrup.

YIELD: 2¼ CUPS

TIP: To make vanilla-flavored simple syrup, add about ½ teaspoon vanilla extract to the syrup once it has cooled. Or if you like peppermint, add ½ teaspoon peppermint extract.

CopyKat.com's **SMASHBURGER®**

Sauce

Smashburger puts together one delicious hamburger. I recommend that you stop there if you like hamburgers that are made to order and taste very close to homemade. One of their specialties there is the Smashburger sauce. It makes a nice change from "secret sauce," and piping-hot French fries taste great dipped in it.

2 teaspoons chopped dill pickle

½ cup mayonnaise

¼ cup prepared yellow mustard

2 teaspoons dill pickle juice

1 teaspoon vegetable oil

In a small bowl, stir together the chopped dill pickle, mayonnaise, mustard, pickle juice, and oil. Cover and refrigerate for a couple of hours before serving.

The dill pickle juice is critical for this recipe. The sauce has a sour tang but not too many pickles, so the juice is what gives it the dill flavor. Refrigerate until ready to use.

YIELD: APPROXIMATELY ¾ CUP

Cinnamon Honey Butter

This cinnamon honey butter tastes so good on rolls served hot from the oven! Use it on French toast or even plain toast to get your morning off to a great start.

½ cup salted butter, softened	2 tablespoons honey
2 tablespoons superfine sugar	1 teaspoon ground cinnamon

Place all the ingredients in a bowl and beat with an electric mixer until you have a uniform mixture. Store any leftover cinnamon honey butter in the refrigerator, covered.

If you don't have superfine sugar, you can use powdered sugar in its place.

YIELD: APPROXIMATELY ¾ CUP

CopyKat.com's

Vanilla Extract

Vanilla extract is easy to make, and you can save so much money by making your own. Vanilla beans can be purchased at large warehouse stores or even online. Add some good-quality vodka, and in a couple of weeks you'll have wonderful vanilla extract. This makes a great gift , too.

2 or 3 vanilla beans   6 to 8 ounces vodka

Using a sharp knife, split open the vanilla beans lengthwise. Place the beans in an airtight lidded container and pour in enough vodka to fully cover them. Put the lid on the container. Store at room temperature and shake the container at room temperature every couple of days for the next several weeks. The extract will darken with age. As you use your vanilla, you can top it off with more vodka. This has a very long shelf life; as long as the vanilla beans are covered with alcohol, the extract will keep almost indefinitely.

YIELD: 6 TO 8 OUNCES

Peppermint Bark

Williams-Sonoma is famous for the peppermint bark it sells at holiday time. Made with high-quality chocolate, it's a rich and creamy peppermint sensation that also comes with a high price tag—out of reach for some of us. With this recipe, though, you can afford to make some for everyone on your gift list. Williams-Sonoma uses Guittard chocolate; if you can't find Guittard, I recommend using Ghirardelli chocolate.

1 (12-ounce) package semisweet chocolate chips	1 tablespoon vegetable shortening or coconut oil
1 teaspoon peppermint oil, divided	½ cup crushed candy canes
1 (12-ounce) package white chocolate chips	

Melt the semisweet chocolate chips in the top of a double boiler over simmering water. While the chocolate is melting, stir in ½ teaspoon of peppermint oil, combining thoroughly. Line a 9 x 13-inch baking dish with waxed paper, leaving plenty of waxed paper overhanging the sides of the dish. Pour the melted chocolate into the lined dish and allow it to set for 30 to 45 minutes at room temperature.

Once the dark chocolate has set, melt the white chocolate chips together with the shortening in a clean double boiler, stirring often. Blend in the remaining ½ teaspoon peppermint oil. Pour the white chocolate over the set dark chocolate layer. Sprinkle on the crushed candy canes, pressing the larger pieces into the chocolate. Let the white chocolate layer set at room temperature; it will take a couple of hours. Remove the bark from the pan by lifting out the waxed paper. Break into pieces and store at room temperature in an airtight container.

YIELD: 10 TO 12 SERVINGS

TIP: I recommend searching out the peppermint oil called for in this recipe rather than using peppermint extract. Sometimes extracts can cause chocolate to have a grainy texture. Make sure you use food-grade peppermint oil.

Favorites

✕✕✕

This chapter includes some of the most popular recipes from my website, so you have the best of CopyKat.com in your hands. With this chapter you'll have all of my readers' favorite dishes. These are the recipes I cherish the most, because people like you have used them time and time again.

Oreo® Cheesecake

You'll love the sweet creaminess of cheesecake blended with the familiar chocolate Oreo flavor. My biggest tip for making cheesecake is to always let all of your ingredients reach room temperature before you begin to assemble them.

CRUST:

2 tablespoons butter, melted, plus more for pan

1½ cups Oreo cookie crumbs (about 23 cookies, finely chopped)

FILLING:

3 (8-ounce) packages cream cheese, at room temperature

1 cup sugar

5 large eggs, at room temperature

2 teaspoons vanilla extract

¼ teaspoon salt

¼ cup all-purpose flour

1 cup sour cream, at room temperature

15 coarsely chopped Oreo cookies, divided

Preheat the oven to 325°F. Butter the bottom and sides of a 9-inch springform pan.

TO MAKE THE CRUST: Mix the 2 tablespoons melted butter with the Oreo crumbs in a small bowl. Press the crumb mixture into the bottom and 1½ inches up the sides of the buttered pan; set aside.

TO MAKE THE FILLING: Using an electric stand mixer on low speed, beat the cream cheese until light and fluffy. Add the sugar gradually and continue beating until thoroughly incorporated. Add the eggs, one at a time, beating after each addition. Add the vanilla, salt, and flour, beating until smooth. Add the sour cream and beat well. Turn off the mixer and use a spoon to stir in 5 coarsely chopped Oreo cookies.

Pour the filling over the crust in the springform pan. Sprinkle the remaining 10 coarsely chopped Oreos across the top. Place pan on the top rack and in the middle of a preheated oven at 325°F and bake for 1 hour. The cheesecake is done when it jiggles just slightly in the middle when the pan is gently shaken. If the cheesecake is very jiggly, bake for an additional 15 minutes. At the end of the baking time, leave the cheesecake in the oven for another hour with the oven door propped open. Remove from the oven and let cool enough to place in the refrigerator, covered, for 24 hours. It's worth the wait—a cheesecake should rest to let the flavor ripen and become enriched.

YIELD: 16 SERVINGS

CopyKat.com's **CHILI'S®**

Skillet Queso

Skillet Queso has been on the menu at Chili's for years, so you know this recipe is the favorite of many diners. This queso is very easy to make. If you need to reheat it later, add a little milk to the mixture and warm it on the stovetop over low heat.

1 (2-pound) block Kraft Velveeta processed cheese, cubed

2 (15-ounce) cans Hormel no-bean chili

corn tortilla chips, for serving

Simply combine the Velveeta and chili in a slow cooker, cover, and heat on low for several hours, or until the Velveeta is melted. For the most accurate texture, mix warm sauce in a blender before serving. Offer heated corn tortilla chips for dipping.

If you want to serve this just like Chili's does, present it in a warmed cast-iron skillet.

YIELD: 24 SERVINGS

CopyKat.com's **CRACKER BARREL OLD COUNTRY STORE®**

Fried Apples

I think you will find this recipe captures the essence of the fried apples served at the Cracker Barrel. For this recipe I actually like to use a variety of apples for the best flavor.

¼ cup bacon drippings, or you can use butter

6 tart apples, cored and sliced (peeled, if desired)

1 teaspoon freshly squeezed lemon juice

¼ cup packed dark brown sugar

⅛ teaspoon salt

1 teaspoon ground cinnamon

dash of grated nutmeg

In a large skillet over low heat, melt the bacon drippings or butter. Scatter the apples evenly over the skillet bottom and sprinkle on the lemon juice. Add the brown sugar and salt. Cover and cook over low heat for 15 minutes, stirring occasionally, until the apples are tender and juicy. Sprinkle with cinnamon and nutmeg to serve.

YIELDS: 8 SERVINGS

Hash Brown Casserole

Whenever I have breakfast at the Cracker Barrel, I order these famous hash browns. These are good as part of any meal, so you don't need to limit them to breakfast. You can prepare this casserole a day ahead up to the point of baking it.

2 tablespoons butter or vegetable oil

1 (2-pound) bag frozen country-style hash browns

½ cup (or so) finely chopped onion

Jane's Krazy Mixed-up Salt, to taste

1½ to 2 cups shredded Colby cheese (I love cheese, but in this case more is not necessarily better)

1 (10-ounce) can condensed cream of chicken soup

Preheat the oven to 350°F. Butter or oil a 9 x 13-inch baking dish.

Heat the butter or oil in a large skillet over medium heat. Add the hash browns, onions, and salt. Cook until the hash browns are tender and brown. Set the hash browns aside while you prepare the sauce. In a bowl, mix the shredded cheese with the cream of chicken soup. Stir in the hash browns, then transfer the mixture to the prepared baking dish. Bake for 30 minutes, or until golden brown.

YIELD: 8 TO 10 SERVINGS

CopyKat.com's HOOTERS™

Fried Pickles

You must be thinking I'm crazy. Fried pickles are fantastic! They're crunchy and tangy. Here we use simple hamburger dill slices. Some places like to fry pickle spears, but I don't like them as well. They aren't crispy, they're soft, and not what I really like. So here are some delicious fried pickles you can serve, and they taste a lot like Hooters fried pickles. You'll have to provide your own Hooters girls to get the total experience.

8 cups vegetable oil, for frying

1 (11-ounce) jar hamburger dill pickle slices

2 cups buttermilk

2 cups whole-wheat flour

1 cup all-purpose flour

2 teaspoons salt

1 teaspoon paprika

¼ teaspoon cayenne pepper

Heat the vegetable oil to 350°F in a large pot. Drain the pickles in a colander and place them in a medium bowl with the buttermilk. Place all the dry ingredients in a separate bowl and mix well.

Take about a handful of pickles out of the buttermilk and dredge in the seasoned flour. Shake off the excess flour and drop the battered pickles into the hot oil and fry until golden brown. Be careful not to put too many pickles in the hot oil at once or they won't crisp. Continue cooking until all the pickles are done. Drain on a wire rack, which will keep the pickles crsip.

YIELD: 4 SERVINGS

CopyKat.com's OLIVE GARDEN®

Salad Dressing

This has to be one of the best-known of any restaurant salad dressings—so popular that the recipe has remained one of my most requested and viewed recipes of all time.

½ cup mayonnaise

⅓ cup white vinegar

1 teaspoon vegetable oil

2 tablespoons light corn syrup

2 tablespoons grated Parmesan cheese

2 tablespoons grated Romano cheese

¼ teaspoon garlic salt, or 1 minced garlic clove garlic

½ teaspoon Italian seasoning

½ teaspoon dried parsley flakes

1 tablespoon freshly squeezed lemon juice

sugar (optional)

Place all the ingredients in a blender and blend until thoroughly mixed. If the dressing is a little too tart for your personal taste, add a little sugar. Serve with the Olive Garden Salad Mix (page 207). Another great use for this dressing is as a marinade for vegetables or meats that you will be grilling.

YIELD: 10 SERVINGS

CopyKat.com's OLIVE GARDEN®

Salad Mix

Now that you have the salad dressing (previous page), it's time to make the salad. I think the Dole American Blend salad mix is perfect to use. If you like to mix things up, change the pepperoncini to banana peppers.

- 1 (12-ounce) bag Dole American Blend salad mix
- 4 or 5 slices red onion
- 4 to 6 pitted black olives
- 2 to 4 pepperoncini (if you like a sweeter pepper, you could use a banana pepper)
- 1 small tomato, quartered
- ½ cup seasoned croutons
- freshly grated Romano cheese (Parmesan works well, too!)

Chill your salad bowl in the freezer for at least 30 minutes. Pour the salad mix into the chilled bowl and top with the onion slices, olives, pepperoncinis, tomato pieces, and croutons. Add some freshly grated cheese, and finish with plenty of Olive Garden Salad Dressing (page 206).

YIELD: 2 TO 3 SERVINGS

CopyKat.com's **OLIVE GARDEN®**

Zuppa Toscana

What's one of the best reasons to make a CopyKat recipe? You get to add more of your favorite ingredients! This soup is filled with potatoes, kale, and Italian sausage. You can substitute spinach for the kale, but in that case I would add the spinach just before serving. Also, I find that Yukon Gold potatoes are a tasty alternative to russets in this soup.

1 pound bulk Italian sausage

¼ to ½ teaspoon crushed red pepper flakes

1 cup chopped onion (about 1 onion)

2 large russet potatoes, halved and cut into ¼ inch slices

2 (14-ounce) cans chicken broth (low-sodium is best)

4 cups water

2 garlic cloves, minced

⅓ cup cooked bacon pieces, or purchased "real bacon bits"

salt and pepper to taste

2 cups chopped kale or Swiss chard

1 cup heavy cream

In a medium skillet, brown the sausage over medium heat. Add the red pepper flakes and continue browning the sausage until it is completely cooked. In a large saucepan or soup pot over medium heat, cook the onion, potatoes, chicken broth, water, and garlic until the potatoes are cooked through. Stir in the cooked sausage along with the bacon, salt, and pepper. Simmer for another 10 minutes, then turn the heat to low and add the chopped kale or chard and the cream. Heat through and serve.

YIELD: 8 SERVINGS

CopyKat.com's WENDY'S®

Chili

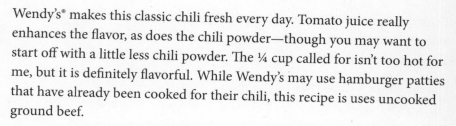

Wendy's® makes this classic chili fresh every day. Tomato juice really enhances the flavor, as does the chili powder—though you may want to start off with a little less chili powder. The ¼ cup called for isn't too hot for me, but it is definitely flavorful. While Wendy's may use hamburger patties that have already been cooked for their chili, this recipe is uses uncooked ground beef.

2 pounds freshly ground beef

4 cups tomato juice

1 (29-ounce) can tomato purée

1 (15-ounce) can red kidney beans, drained and rinsed

1 (15-ounce) can pinto beans, drained and rinsed

1 medium onion, chopped (about 1½ cups)

½ cup diced celery

¼ cup diced green bell pepper

¼ cup chili powder (or less, to taste)

1 teaspoon ground cumin (if you like its distinctive flavor, add more)

1½ teaspoons garlic powder

1 teaspoon salt

½ teaspoon ground black pepper

½ teaspoon dried oregano

½ teaspoon sugar

⅛ teaspoon cayenne pepper

In a skillet, brown the ground beef, breaking it up with a spoon, then drain off the fat. Transfer the beef and the remaining ingredients to a 6-quart soup pot and add all the remaining ingredients. Cover and let the chili simmer for 1 to 1½ hours over low heat, stirring every 15 minutes. (You can also cook this in a slow cooker on low for 3 to 4 hours.)

YIELD: 10 SERVINGS

Cheddar Bay Biscuits™

It's hard to turn down hot bread, especially when it's topped with butter and garlic. Now you don't have to leave home to enjoy them. These fluffy biscuits have been a website favorite for a long time.

2 cups Bisquick baking mix

½ cup cold water

¾ cup shredded sharp Cheddar cheese

¼ cup (½ stick) butter

1 teaspoon dried parsley flakes

½ teaspoon garlic powder

½ teaspoon Italian seasoning

Preheat the oven to 350°F. In a bowl, mix together the Bisquick, water, and shredded cheese. Turn the biscuits onto a floured service and roll out the dough to ½ inch thick. Cut the dough with a biscuit cutter and place the biscuits on a baking sheet about 2 inches apart. Bake for 8 to 10 minutes, or until the tops are golden brown.

Meanwhile, melt the butter with the seasonings in a small saucepan over low heat. Remove the lightly browned biscuits from the oven, brush the tops with the seasoned butter, and serve immediately.

YIELD: 8 TO 10 BISCUITS, ABOUT 4 SERVINGS

Handy Conversions

1 tablespoon .... 3 teaspoons

1 cup .... 16 tablespoons

1 pint .... 2 cups

1 quart .... 2 pints

1 gallon .... 4 quarts

1 pound .... 16 ounces

1 stick butter .... ½ cup / 8 ounces

1 ounce butter .... 2 tablespoons

Metric Conversions

1 teaspoon .... 5 milliliters

1 tablespoon .... 15 milliliters

1 cup .... 240 milliliters

2 cups .... 470 milliliters

4 cups .... 0.95 liter

4 quarts .... 3.8 liters

1 fluid ounce .... 30 milliliters / 28 grams

1 ounce .... 28 grams

1 pound .... 454 grams

350°F / 400°F .... 175°F / 200°C

Recipe Index

Recipe Index

by Restaurant

CARRABBA'S ITALIAN GRILL®
Chicken Bryan, 71

CHACHO'S™
Mango Salsa, 22

CHEDDAR'S CASUAL CAFE®
Santa Fe Dip, 23
Sweet Corn off the Cob, 105
Texas Cheese Fries, 24
Cajun Café™
Bourbon Chicken, 70

THE CHEESECAKE FACTORY®
Oreo® Cheesecake, 200

CHILI'S®
Skillet Queso, 202

COCO'S BAKERY RESTAURANT®
Nutella™ Crêpes, 135

COLD STONE CREAMERY®
Cake Batter Ice Cream®, 136

CRACKER BARREL OLD COUNTRY STORE®
Broccoli Cheddar Chicken, 72
Chocolate Pecan Pie, 137
Fried Apples, 203
Hash Brown Casserole, 204
Pumpkin Custard N' Ginger Snap, 138
Sawmill Gravy, 168
Sunday Chicken, 73

DAIRY QUEEN®
Banana Split Blizzard®, 140
Chocolate Covered Cherry Blizzard®, 141
Dude, 74
Peanut Butter Parfait Bar, 142
Turtlette Blizzard®, 143

RED LOBSTER®
Buffalo Chicken Bites, 39
Cheddar Bay Biscuits™, 210
Shrimp Nachos, 40

SALTGRASS STEAKHOUSE®
Boiled Shrimp and Avocado Salsa, 41
Chicken Tenders, 94
Lemon Pepper Zucchini, 42
Range Rattlers™, 43

SMASHBURGER®
Sauce, 195

SOUP PLANTATION & SWEET TOMATOES®
Creamy Herbed Turkey Soup, 65
Lemon Greek Penne Pasta, 122
Roasted Mushroom Soup with Sage, 66

SPAGHETTI WAREHOUSE®
Classic Bruschetta, 47
Sausage and Mozzarella Bruschetta, 48

SONIC®
Mozzarella Cheese Sticks, 45
Root Beer Freeze, 15
Ultimate Meat & Cheese™ Breakfast Burrito, 183
Vanilla Coke, 14

STAR PIZZA™
Goat Cheese and Roasted Garlic, 46

STARBUCKS™
Eggnog Latte, 16
Pumpkin Bread, 182
Pumpkin Spice Latte, 17

SUBWAY®
Orchard Chicken Salad, 95

MISCELLANEOUS

About the Author

※※※※※※※※※※※※※※※※※※※※※※※

Stephanie Manley is the creator and author of CopyKat.com. Since 1995, she has written recipes for restaurant-style dishes that anyone can make in their own kitchen. While working in restaurants, Stephanie began to write restaurant-style recipes to help save money and stretch her budget. Like many people, she couldn't afford to go out for dinner every night of the week, but wanted to re-create the taste of her favorite dishes at home. CopyKat.com, known for its trustworthy and delicious recipes, is now one of the internet's most popular cooking websites, and has been featured in publications like the *Wall Street Journal*, *Newsweek*, and *Woman's World*. Find Stephanie online at www.CopyKat.com or www.twitter.com/CopyKatRecipes. She lives in Kingwood, Texas.